WE'VE ALL DONE IT

Getting **Real** about the Role We Each Play in a **Toxic Workplace**

Kimberly J. Benoit

WE'VE ALL DONE IT

First edition 2023

www.kimberlyjbenoit.com
kb@kimberlyjbenoit.com

ISBN: 979-8-9871320-0-5 (eBook)
ISBN: 979-8-9871320-1-2 (paperback)
ISBN: 979-8-9871320-2-9 (hardcover)

Printed in the United States of America

Editor: Jodi Brandon
Cover and Book Design: Melissa Williams Design
Photograph: Karen Moreau

KIM'S NON-LEGAL DISCLAIMER

Imitation is the sincerest form of flattery
that mediocrity can pay to greatness.

~Oscar Wilde

This book is intended to take you on a self-reflective professional journey. Together, we will create
self-awareness of our own toxic leadership tendencies.
There are no solutions in this book, as we can't focus
on what to do until we fully understand what has been
and is today. Also, solutions are personal and must take
into account all of our unique circumstances (e.g., race,
gender identity, role, company culture, etc.). Before we
get to a development plan, we really need to understand
how we have showed and are showing up for our teams.
This book is that first step.

The scenarios presented in this book are a compila-
tion of personal experiences, professional observations,
and insights by myself, my peers, and clients I've worked
with. Throughout my more than 20 years of corporate
life, leadership, and coaching, I have distilled several
common themes into seven scenarios. The characters and
situations presented within these scenarios are a combi-

nation of people and experiences. No scenario is based off a single person or event.

If you see yourself in some way within these pages and scenarios, congratulations! You're in great company. I don't know a single person (regardless of race, gender, industry, etc.) who hasn't experienced at least one aspect of one of the scenarios in this book. If you're a leader, you have either experienced or witnessed many of these. If you're a new leader and this seems a bit foreign, hold on. You will. It's almost a guarantee.

I want to reiterate that you might feel strong emotions throughout the upcoming pages. The beta readers of this book sure did and asked me to include a special warning for you. The pages in this book will remind you of times when you have taken actions you are not proud of or when you were the recipient of less-than-stellar leadership. They will stir very strong emotions in you.

I hope that when you recognize yourself in these pages you will use it as an opportunity to reflect on the situation you were in, your role in that situation, and how you grew from it. Maybe even reflect on what you would do differently in the same situation now.

Just to make you feel better, I remind you that I'm in this book too. In almost every scenario, there is some aspect of my lived experience mixed in with others. As unique as we all are, we all live through similar experiences. I hope this provides an opportunity for you to see yourself and be proud of who you are—but also to see that we all have more learning and growing to do.

To Karoma & Sarah

CONTENTS

Gratitude XI

Introduction 1

Chapter 1: Toxicity & Why it Matters 9

Chapter 2: I Swear it Isn't Me 22

Chapter 3: What's That Smell? 27

Chapter 4: Walk the Talk 40

Chapter 5: Fear and Loathing in the Office 53

Chapter 6: I'm Pretty Sure I Am God 65

Chapter 7: Where My Single People At? 75

Chapter 8: You've Got a Friend in Me 86

Chapter 9: Can You Hear Me Now? 100

Conclusion 112

Discussion Guide 117

Chapter Notes 125

Resources 127

About the Author 131

GRATITUDE

Praise You Like I Should

*Let us be grateful to the people who make us happy;
they are the charming gardeners who make
our souls blossom.*

~Marcel Proust

To everyone whose eyes lit up when I talked about this idea for a book. To all of those who openly shared stories to ensure the book captured real and relatable experiences. Your courage and vulnerability are inspiring and have made this journey worth it.

To those who have worked with me, worked for me, or (God bless you) led me—Thank you for pushing me and helping me to be a better leader and person. It wasn't always pretty but hopefully it's been worth it.

To Elizabeth Gilbert—*Big Magic* is why this book was written. Thank you for the continued inspiration.

To my beta readers, Michelle Argyle, and Jodi Brandon—Your dedication, insights, and encouragement have meant everything.

To Jacq and the MOFO family—Thank you for helping me believe that I could do this and for helping to see myself as a writer.

To Nancy, Allyson, Rochelle, Kristen, and the Bears—Thank you for challenging me to not play small. For seeing more in me than I could see in myself. Most importantly, for providing a supportive, yet constant drumbeat to be my best self.

To my family by choice (Erin, Jaime, Kevin, Diane, Amy, Susan, Heather, Ashleigh, Lora, Julia, and many more)—Thank you for your unending support and, more importantly, the reality checks. You keep me grounded and keep me going. Never enough words to say thank you.

To the family that is stuck with me—You have seen me through all of the times—good, bad, and ugly. Thank you for continuing to show up and support me no matter how crazy the idea.

INTRODUCTION

You can't change who you've been. It's never too late to
choose who you want to become.

~ Adam Grant

How This All Began

As with any great story, it all began over drinks with
a friend. More like a bitch session, if you will. We
were talking about a leader we both knew who we liked
personally but would never work for. In essence, they were
a sweet person but an absolute doormat of a leader. They
hated confrontation and had issues with turnover because
poor performers were never really held accountable.
Drama was the culture on that team despite the leader's
best efforts. As much as we liked them personally, they
were a bit toxic. We even said, "I bet they don't even know
how toxic they are."

After another glass of wine and some appetizers, a
thought occurred to me. I wondered how many of my

current and former employees would describe me as toxic. It took less than a millisecond for a person's face to appear in my mind. She was an average-at-best employee who thought she was exceptional and demanded privileges and rewards far beyond what she deserved. She thought I was unfair and biased for not seeing her brilliance. From her perspective, I was a terrible leader.

Upon reflection, I felt confident that, despite what this person thought, I did the right things and I showed up as the best leader I could with the leadership experience I had. The reason she hated me is because I held her accountable when her performance was subpar. I didn't allow her to slide and, to her, I was mean and vindictive. Could I have handled things differently? I can say with the experience I have now that, yes, I would likely do a few things differently. Would that change how this person feels about me and that situation? Possibly, but I am guessing not. Clearly, perspective matters.

All of this got me thinking and asking myself all kinds of questions:

- Do leaders know when they're being toxic?
- Do I know when I'm being toxic?
- What makes a leader truly toxic versus a leader who just screwed up?
- Can toxic leaders change?

Then I started really thinking about myself. When have I been a legitimately toxic leader or done things that could feel toxic to others? In those less-than-stellar moments, what would I go back and change now that I have awareness and know more? Are there triggers that could lead me to engage in toxic leadership behaviors again?

In the subsequent days and weeks, I started asking other colleagues and pretty much anyone I encountered if they had had a toxic leader. Most were quick to start naming names. Frequently, they asked how much time I had and couldn't wait to tell me a story. Then I asked how many of their current or former employees would label them as a toxic leader. Again, chuckles ensued because they had lists of names there, too, but the conversation was different because most felt that these were unfair beliefs. Some admitted that they could have done better and would likely do things differently in hindsight, but they had never meant to be toxic.

After several weeks of recurring thoughts and new questions about toxic behavior and toxic leadership, I realized I needed to do something. This is when I started putting words to paper. I honestly didn't set out to write a book. But in the days and weeks following that one social gathering, this idea kept reappearing in my life.

Elizabeth Gilbert, of *Eat, Pray, Love* fame, also wrote a book called *Big Magic,* which contains a theory that creativity is a living thing. Basically, ideas are living things looking for someone to nourish them and give them life. This idea of good leaders who maybe don't know they are engaging in toxic behaviors, or that a leader could do all the right things and still be viewed as a toxic leader, really stuck with me. I felt like the universe was calling me to pay attention. Clearly, I had tapped into something. I still did not intend to write a book, but many months and words later here we are. Big magic, indeed.

The Journey We Are Taking Together

As this book began to take shape, I wanted to focus on the self-reflection and self-improvement all leaders need. Initially, I intended to focus on the role of leaders, but then realized all people have skin in this game—whether we are dishing it out, receiving it, or simply observing it. We are human.

When facing any situation, we all bring a plate of something to the potluck—or, as I like to say, some bullshit to the buffet. The real questions are: How big is the plate of bullshit, and how badly is it stinking up the place? Today it might be an amuse-bouche. Tomorrow could be the main course with multiple side dishes. Another way to think about it is we all have our own baggage that colors the way we approach and respond to each other. This book primarily focuses on leaders and their actions, but there's also attention to how even the most casual of observers can, and often do, play a role in creating or sustaining a toxic environment. Every choice we make can either assist in encouraging or eliminating toxic workplace drama.

Leading is not for the weak. There are no "easy" buttons, nor a single answer for how to be a good leader. Initially, many of us think we are good, or at least decent, leaders. But have you ever asked yourself, "Have I been a toxic leader?" or "Does my team think I'm toxic?"

I'm going to cut to the chase: The quick answer to these questions is *yes*. And also *no*.

Even the best leaders have moments or periods of toxicity. We have all been guilty of not showing up as our best selves or in some kind of biased way—whether or not we intend to.

What differentiates a truly toxic leader from a good leader is not someone who is perfect. It is the person who does the best they can, reflects on how they showed up, and commits to changing when they realize just maybe they could have done better. It is the ability to recognize when you have failed or are failing those you serve. I'm not talking about the occasional misstep. I am talking about the times where you actually believe you're showing up in the right way but are actually creating a toxic or unhealthy environment and culture.

Admitting a screw-up is hard for most of us. Honestly, doing so is not always overwhelmingly welcomed in the corporate world, as it could put you or your organization at risk. But the truth is, we are human and will make mistakes. Especially when we are new leaders. Allow this to be a place where admitting your mistakes is not only welcomed, but expected. No one is judging because this space is just for you.

Good leadership is hard. We are all trying to balance the people, policies, and politics of our organizations while maintaining a healthy personal life. That is no easy task in today's challenging environment. However, for me, leading others has provided some of the most rewarding and most challenging times in my life. The truth is that real leadership is some of the hardest work you will ever do. You will fail often. Usually in the presence of others. Specifically, those you're tasked with leading. This why leadership books keep getting written. It's all about helping each other on this journey.

Again, this book (and the subsequent conversation) is not about judgment. It's a place for us to do some real work together about who we are as leaders.

Let's Get Started!

I challenge you to be really honest with yourself about who you are as a leader and how you're showing up for others. You will be frustrated at times because there are scenarios that may feel like you're looking in a mirror. That's okay. In these moments, slow down and ask more questions about why this is frustrating you. What's coming up for you at that moment? This is where the real work takes place.

I won't ask anything of you that I have not asked of myself. In every word I've written, I have reflected on my own leadership journey and come to some realizations about where I could and will do better in the future. This is the point: the willingness to say that you have screwed up, even if just a little bit. It's okay to only declare this to yourself. Take the time to really be honest and then forgive yourself on the path to being the leader you want to be— and that your team deserves.

This book focuses on how we can all be susceptible to faults that create negative environments for those we lead. The goal here is to talk about the challenges of leading others with compassion, humility, and humor at the forefront.

Here's what I need from you on this self-reflective journey: I need you to be open minded, to get uncomfortable, to laugh at yourself, and to ask yourself a few hard questions—questions like:

- What aspects of this scenario resonate with me?
- Have I done something like this in the past?
- Would I do this again, or would I make different choices?

If you have gone through the trouble to get this book and start reading it, I'm hopeful that you will walk through this process with me. If it was gifted to you, maybe someone is being a friend and trying to help you navigate a tough moment right now.

I just ask that you don't give up. Do anything else, like . . . get mad. Take a break. But come back and keep reading. Keep asking questions and exploring. Just don't give up. We have work to do, and people need us to show up as our best selves. Through a bunch of self-compassion, a little humility, and a lot of laughter, we can get through this together. You ready? Let's go!

CHAPTER 1

Toxicity and Why it Matters

When a workplace becomes toxic, its poison spreads beyond
its walls and into the lives of its workers and their families.

~ Gary Chapman

Let's be honest. You know it when you see it. More
likely, you know it when you feel it. Being around
someone in a toxic state leaves me feeling icky, drained,
cynical, bitter, and (many times) angry. Because they're in
a negative space, that energy spreads to those they interact with, especially those they lead. If you are an intui-
tive person, this could be incredibly damaging, as it is so
easy to absorb those emotions and energies, leading to you
potentially carrying that negative feeling forward, perpet-
uating the toxicity.

In researching for this book, I was taken aback by
Google's immediately suggested list of toxic leaders: Adolf
Hitler, Joseph Stalin, Attila the Hun. Although a bit more

extreme than what I was looking for, and hopefully not representative of a toxic leader you've encountered, Google definitely makes a point. At the extreme of toxicity, the ramifications are unforeseen and long-lasting, and destroy people's lives beyond the immediate. When looking at it on a more personal level, having a toxic leader or getting caught up in a toxic environment can also have long-lasting effects—and can definitely derail careers and lives.

Let's Define *Toxic*

According to the trusty *Merriam-Webster* dictionary, *toxic* is defined as "containing or being poisonous material especially when capable of causing death or serious debilitation" or "extremely harsh, malicious, or harmful."[1] I don't know about you, but those words just hit pretty hard. *Poisonous. Harmful. Extremely harsh.* How many times have you used those words to describe one of your leaders? Better yet, how many times have those words been used to describe you as a leader?

Okay, I'm getting a bit ahead of myself, but the interesting thing about toxic people is that they frequently aren't aware they are indeed toxic or that their actions are feeding a toxic culture. Often, they think it's someone else, or that they're just part of a bad situation. Our goal in this book is to slow down and really understand what toxicity looks like in general, how it might look for each of us, and what we want to do once we see ourselves differently.

Why Toxic Leaders Matter

Before we get into the research and data around toxic leadership, take a few minutes to close your eyes and picture the faces of all the great leaders you have had in your career. Go ahead and close your eyes. I'll wait.

What emotions came up for you when you thought about these people? Joy? Respect? Admiration? Happiness? Gratitude? What made them great leaders? Really think about this because it's important to understand why someone we admire and respect earns that distinction. What specific behaviors or traits made these people great leaders?

Again close your eyes, but this time envision every leader you felt was toxic. It doesn't matter if it was a direct leader or someone you interacted with. Take a few moments. Again, I'm a patient person.

Feeling your blood pressure go up just at the thought of their names and faces? I mean, chances are you have had more than one. I know I have. Again, what feelings came up for you? Did you notice a literal shift in your body? I do when I think about some of my former leaders or leaders I interacted with.

This simple exercise illustrates why it matters. We can look at all the data in the world, but it's the feeling you are sitting with right now that determines who you want to work for and why. This feeling will determine your success and the likelihood of how *you* show up every day.

I know I said the data is not as important as the feelings, but it does tell a compelling story. In 2022, MIT Sloan published data looking at the top-five predictors of turnover during the Great Resignation.[2] What they found should not surprise anyone, but it's staggering. Their research showed that a toxic culture was the leading factor in people quitting. In fact, a toxic corporate culture was **10.4 times** more powerful than compensation in predicting a company's attrition rate compared with its industry. Let that sink in: 10 times!

Who we are as leaders and how we show up are leading indicators of the health of not only our individual teams, but the company overall. The only way we can get better and grow is through self-reflection. It's by having that uncomfortable conversation with ourselves. After asking some tough questions, we may find we have done all we could and we are doing a good job. We might also find situations where we were the ones bringing the stinky pile to the proverbial buffet.

Types of Toxic Leaders

Not all toxic leaders are the same. Their impacts may be similar, but recognizing how they got there might be helpful in understanding how we, as leaders, can end up there too. This doesn't excuse poor behavior but it does put things in perspective. It can also help explain why some leaders are hated by some and absolutely loved by others.

I don't want this to seem like I'm letting anyone off the hook, but I think it's important to realize that there's a big difference between someone who has a truly damaging personality (e.g., a narcissist) versus someone who might be going through a rough time in life (e.g., someone going through a divorce, family illness, or role transition).

Let's take a moment to look at each type and better understand who they are and why they are that way. I have found there are two scenarios that tend to play out when looking at toxicity: intentional (personality or blind spot) or situational. Let's look at each of these a bit more.

INTENTIONAL

Intentionally toxic leaders can't help themselves (well, maybe). It's just who they are. It may be their personality (looking at you, my narcissists!). Others could have learned behaviors that have served them well so far, and they are likely not interested or motivated to change even if they are deemed toxic. If you're like me, you have a few faces coming to mind. They can be people who show up through intimidation or fear. They may feel like bullies or, quite frankly, bulldozers because you feel completely run over when interacting with them.

An example that comes to mind is Susan, a mid-level leader who has a turnover problem but consistently leads a team that gets stuff done. The reason there's a turnover problem is because Susan believes all of the team's success is due to her brilliance in hiring the right people and guiding the team to execution. She never credits the team, and she believes her way is the best way. Unfortunately, most new employees don't figure this out until after they've joined and have been successful in their roles, only to never be given the credit they deserve.

In these situations, change is difficult because many of the toxic behaviors are actually part of the leader's success. On paper, Susan gets things done and hires great people, even if they don't stay on her team long term. Leaders who have these tendencies will not likely let those toxic behaviors go easily, because they have helped them be successful in their careers.

* * *

Blind spots! We all have them. You know there are always areas where we have soft spots for people or projects that just completely cloud our judgment. We believe we're seeing things super clearly and are making very smart-headed decisions. However, those around us normally have their heads in their hands out of frustration. I can almost hear people screaming internally, "*How could they be so blind?*"

In case you need an example because you are super awesome and don't have any blind spots, this is for you.

There's a team with a leader who tends to favor a longer-serving employee over other team members because that one person has stayed and has been loyal to her throughout the years. This might include overlooking when this employee underperforms, creating an inequity in how she holds team members accountable. Ultimately, there are engagement and turnover issues as people get frustrated that the leader's favoritism affects her ability to see clearly and have consistent standards on the team. We know through the tremendous work of Cy Wakeman, a leading voice in leadership and ego research, that accountability matters.[3] When we, as leaders, have blind spots and create exceptions for those we like, we're definitely part of the problem—even though we think we're doing a good thing.

SITUATIONAL

Situationally toxic leaders happen. Situational toxicity happens when something happens in life and someone just is not showing up as their best. What comes to mind is when a person has been assigned a large stressful project while going through a difficult divorce. There's no solid ground here. Lots of stress, but not all of these things will last forever.

Also, think of burnout, massive life changes, or work changes that create some kind of squeeze on a person. It's all too much for a leader at that moment. And that moment can last a day, a week, a month, or even longer. For many, the recent pandemic created incredibly challenged environments that stressed even the best of us. Suddenly remote work, homeschooling, an unstable job market, social isolation, *no toilet paper,* and the possibility of dying from a new virus could push any sane person over the edge.

I am going to get a bit vulnerable (thank you, Brené Brown!) and use a personal story for this example. In one of my corporate roles, I was responsible for a multi-million-dollar program and was facing some challenges with a few stakeholders. In a meeting with my boss, I was having a rough day, to the point that my then-leader stopped me mid-sentence and told me I was shrill. I needed to tone it down because my approach was part of the problem, not the stakeholders.

Talk about a gut punch. I immediately was angry. How could she not see my side? What was she talking about? I mean, me, be shrill? *Never!*

What people didn't know was that my marriage was falling apart and I was really struggling with the knowledge that divorce was on the horizon. I am a pretty private person and no one at work knew. It wasn't until I got some pretty direct and candid feedback that I realized the strain of what was happening at home was completely manifesting in my interactions at work.

After I was able to calm down (and, yes, vent to a friend), I realized I didn't have it all under control and was projecting some of my internal strife onto the work situation. I started to see a therapist because I knew I needed more support to navigate it all. Staying the course was not an option.

Even situational toxicity is hard on those around you. In these moments, whatever is toxic tends to resolve as the situation evolves. With the pandemic as an example, people began to adapt. Flexible work hours became more of the norm so people could be present for their children and still be able to get their work done. I saw incredible generosity when someone clearly was at the end of their rope, knowing this one moment or month didn't define who they were. It was just the situation.

Now, Let's Get to Work

Now that we've taken a walk down memory lane of leaders we've worked with, this is where I want you to put that mirror up and take a look at yourself. Let me clarify something: Not only have we been the recipient of toxic leadership at some point in our career, but we have likely been a toxic leader to someone. Throughout the journey we go on in this book, we look at various kinds of toxic leadership, being honest about what it looks like, including assessing various real-life scenarios.

From there, we break down the situation and look at it from various angles, looking at what could be considered toxic and possible alternate actions that could have been taken. However, I won't have all the answers. If I did, I would be retired in the south of France, enjoying my work-free life and consuming all of the wine and cheese. Ultimately, answers about what to do and what to change about yourself lie within you. Every situation has its own nuances and considerations. Only you will know all of the circumstances, and there is no one answer to any of these situations that will magically solve all of your problems. It just doesn't work that way, and anyone saying they have all the answers is likely not being honest.

Upcoming chapters in the book present a series of seven scenarios. We zoom in on various work situations that may look and feel familiar to you. After each scenario is a series of questions to help process what you've read and, ultimately, help you reflect on what is familiar to you in these examples. What I'm asking may be hard at times because it might churn up some tough emotions. That's okay. Keep going through it.

Remember, the work you are doing in these reflective sections is for your eyes and heart only, especially the Self-Reflection Exercise section at the end of each scenario presented. This isn't for book club. (If you want that, check out the Discussion Guide at the end of the book.) Use the questions within each chapter to go deep with yourself. Embrace the hard feelings that come up—and, I promise you, they will. Use this as a time to reflect, forgive, and decide how you want to move forward.

These scenarios serve to highlight common areas where people falter as leaders. Not every leader will struggle in all of these areas, but it's normal that you will either struggle in this yourself and/or see someone else struggle with these various leadership situations. Here's a brief overview of the scenarios.

WHAT'S THAT SMELL?

We start here because I have a feeling we've all been here. It's when you are so burned out that you can no longer be objective. From decision-making to basic day-to-day management, you're missing things—not seeing people or situations clearly. As a result, you aren't reacting in the way you would prefer.

WALK THE TALK

We have all heard them: Brené Brown. Simon Sinek. Adam Grant. We've all been guilty of spurting their words in moments when our own fail us. Their words are powerful in their simplicity. The challenge comes when we, as leaders, lean on these inspirational words but our actions don't actually live up to them.

FEAR AND LOATHING IN THE OFFICE

This is the moment your fear of angering someone or of confrontation outweighs your ability to actually lead. This includes not holding people accountable because you don't want to deal with the fight and the anger that will ensue.

I'M PRETTY SURE I AM GOD

I consider this the power trip leader. The ultimate narcissist. The one who believes there is no one better at their world than they are. They are not to be challenged. They are often the veterans of a company or a team. They get frustrated when people want to introduce change before they think it's wise.

WHERE MY SINGLE PEOPLE AT?

This gets into the biases that exist pertaining to relationship and parental status. For instance, the thought that single people don't need as much money as someone who is married with kids, or that someone can take on more work because they don't have as many home responsibilities. It's about the slippery slope of assumption.

YOU'VE GOT A FRIEND IN ME

I hate to say this, but I've seen this more times than I care to count. It has been the spark to so many people choosing to leave teams because leaders valued the wrong thing. Essentially, they promote the people they trust. Sometimes it's a friend. When you value loyalty over performance, you keep getting loyalty, but maybe not from the team members from whom you need it most.

CAN YOU HEAR ME NOW?

Here we look at a leader who uses their voice as a tool of intimidation, and how that affects their ability to work with others and maintain an engaged team.

* * *

In *No Ego*, Cy Wakeman says a leader, at times, needs to stop believing everything they think. You need to suspend your own assumptions and biases to do real self-reflective work. This is what I'm asking you to do. Don't believe everything you think. You might be surprised at what comes up. As she brilliantly states, "The philosophy is self-study, asking yourself about yourself, getting quiet and thinking about the answers, finding clarity about what is true and where the narrator in your head is leading you astray."[4] Take this time to really do the hard work of seeing more clearly versus what your ego wants to believe to be true, which is that you're completely innocent.

You will face questions like "Where in these descriptions have you seen yourself?" It's okay to be honest. There isn't a test or a roll call taking place. Be 100% truthful. Do you see yourself in those scenarios? In what way? How often are you toxic and in what way? Are you making your peers and your team members miserable and not realizing until now that you're doing it?

I will fess up and say *yes*, I've been guilty of a few of the behaviors described in this book. Maybe more than once. We've all engaged in some of these toxic behaviors at some point.

It's natural and okay. We are all human. The challenge here is to recognize it and then *do something* about it.

Being a real leader means deciding to change to be a better person and leader. It's acknowledging what has happened or is currently happening and choosing to do better. Because we must. Our teams are depending on it.

CHAPTER 2

I Swear it Isn't Me

It's not denial. I'm just selective about the reality I accept.

~ Bill Watterson

Let's address the elephant in the room, because I can feel the collective eye rolls out there.

> "But Kim, I'm a good leader. It isn't fair to blame me."
>
> "Some employees just push buttons."
>
> "No matter what I did, we didn't click. They just drove me crazy."
>
> "Kim, my leadership wasn't the problem. They were just a bad fit."
>
> "He was a terrible employee."
>
> "Her attitude really sucked. She was just a pain in the ass."

What I'm hearing you say is "It wasn't me. It was them." I can almost hear the heavy breathing and the scream of—"

> "I was **not** the toxic one. **They were!!** *They just chose to take things wrong and pushed all the wrong buttons. They brought the toxicity to the team.* **Not me!**"
>
> "*Seriously, what is a good leader supposed to do when you have someone who is just not working out and making your life and the lives of your team miserable?*"

Well, the hard answer is not the easy answer. You are supposed to be the "adult" in the room. You're supposed to lead. You aren't supposed to get caught up in the drama.

Now before you slam this book closed and tell me where to go and how to get there, *I am not judging you!* I will fully own that I have fallen into this trap myself.

I have said all of these words, many times. I know the frustration of trying everything and still nothing is working. The dread of yet another resistant, negative encounter with someone who just wants to stir the pot of conflict. Almost as if their life depends on it. I know the frustration of wanting to be a good leader in the face of a challenging employee and walking away feeling completely deflated.

The reality is, whether we intend it or not, we're playing a role in this drama. A good leader's job is to know this and to have enough self-awareness and vulnerability to admit to what they're bringing to the table. The truth is you may be doing your best. You may not be adding fuel to any fire.

But you won't know this unless you ask the right questions. The important part is to ask yourself the questions and be honest about what is really happening.

Let's Look in the Mirror

Let's take a moment and walk down memory lane. Picture the face of an employee (or two) who you *know* considers you a toxic leader. If you're anything like me, this isn't that hard of a task and likely took seconds. We all have someone who pretty much thinks we are a version of Satan.

Now put yourself in their mindset. Pretend to be them for a few moments and try to see the world through their eyes—even if you think they are wrong. Picture one of your interactions with them. Really embody their worldview and what was happening in their world at that moment. Allow yourself to feel the emotions they would have been feeling. I know this might be hard, but just allow yourself to go there.

This can be a fun exercise once you embrace the process because you are likely taking the extreme view of this person's thoughts and behaviors. But I encourage you to suspend your feelings and judgments at this moment. Really get into their headspace and try to see yourself through their perspective.

- What was that like for you?
- What emotions came up for you?
- Were the emotions you felt different when viewing the situation from their perspective?

Now, let's take a slightly different view. Allow yourself to be a fly on the wall. See yourself and this employee as if you are watching a reality TV show. What do you notice about your body language? What about theirs? What about the words each of you are saying?

With this lens, let's consider a couple more questions:

- From the perspective of the employee, how would you describe yourself as a leader?

- What emotions came up for you?

Now that I have your blood pressure up again, I want you to go a bit deeper. No groaning—this is the work!

With this new perspective after taking yourself out of your seat and really challenging yourself to see a situation with new eyes, was there anything *from their perspective* that might have been valid? What words or actions were fueling a toxic dynamic? By them? By you? Were you bringing some BS to the table, whether you intended to or not? Be honest! Were any of their negative feelings or toxic experiences with you valid?

I know this is tough. Trust me. I've done this work and I know it isn't fun or easy. Without any hesitation, I can tell you there are several former employees who see my face when they think of a toxic leader. Was I really toxic? Maybe. But the reality is they think I was to them.

At this point, it isn't about whether I agree. It's about being reflective and honest about what I brought to the table in those moments, and challenging myself to see how I fed the situation. The reality is that I found times when I know I showed up the best I could and was not feeding a toxic culture, regardless of another person's experience. But the harder moment is when I have found that

I did indeed feed the proverbial beast. I was a part of the problem whether I intended to be or not.

What I'm asking you to do is to ask these hard questions of yourself. Before throwing up your hands and simply saying there was nothing you could do and that they were just going to see you as a villain, let's really ask the questions:

- Were you the villain at that moment?

- Was there any possible truth to what that employee was feeling and experiencing?

- Were you being a toxic leader?

The truth is that you may come back with a resounding *no*. You did everything you could and showed up in all the right ways. You might also, upon reflection, come back with a slightly different lens. Time and space may allow you to see that maybe—just maybe—you were part of the problem.

We are human! Leaders are not superheroes, and we make mistakes. The only way we can learn and grow is by taking the time to reflect and be honest about who we were and how we showed up. This is the only way to have a chance of showing up as a better version of ourselves in the future.

As you progress through this book, I challenge you to ask yourself the tough questions. In each chapter, don't just see the faces of others. Really challenge yourself to see if your behavior is reflected in any of these situations. Only by knowing your own patterns and tendencies can you prepare for when they arise again in the future, because as long as you are a leader they will.

CHAPTER 3

What's That Smell?

Burn, if you must
But rise from the dust

~ Parul Nigam

The Setup

Let's be honest. Being around a person, especially a leader, who is burned out isn't all that pleasant. More importantly, their behavior can be contagious or rub off on those around them. It can leave you feeling drained, stressed, and irritable. Honestly, they can make you feel burned out by proxy.

Burnout in the business world is a hot topic and has been for a long time. The term was first used by Dr. Herbert Freudenbeuger in 1980. The term and the reality of burnout have only gained momentum since then with no signs of going away. The American way is one of hustle and grind. The only way to be successful is to work hard and then work harder than that.

The World Health Organization (WHO) defines burnout as "a syndrome conceptualized as resulting from chronic workplace stress that has not been successfully managed. It is characterized by three dimensions:

- feelings of energy depletion or exhaustion;

- increased mental distance from one's job, or feelings of negativism or cynicism related to one's job; and

- reduced professional efficacy.

Burn-out refers specifically to phenomena in the occupational context and should not be applied to describe experiences in other areas of life."[5]

Note that the WHO completely ties burnout to occupational stress and not any other areas of life. Fascinating, but I disagree. There are other aspects of life, when coupled with work, that might be included such as parenting challenges, caring for a sick relative, or just being overwhelmed by personal happenings. For instance, *Merriam-Webster* defines it as "exhaustion of physical or emotional strength or motivation usually as a result of prolonged stress or frustration."[6] Ultimately, it's the overall overwhelm and pressures of life. It can happen to any of us.

Let's be honest. You can't get on any social media platform today without being bombarded with memes for addressing, laughing at, or overcoming burnout. From a more personal sense, we all know burnout when we see it.

However, we can sometimes be blind to how far down we are, not realizing how burned out we are until it's too late.

It doesn't help that burnout can present differently in different people. The symptoms can be very personal and unique to each person. For some, it may include getting sick often, chronic headaches, and being short-tempered. For others, it could look like withdrawal from challenges or people, being overly cynical, and procrastinating. It could also include overworking, a loss of boundaries, and a loss of optimism. It could be one or a combination of any of these. The most important point to note is that these symptoms may pop up occasionally for all of us. Where it moves into burnout territory is when it becomes longer term or chronic. A single day or a week of vacation won't fix it.

As a leader, managing your burnout is critical because your actions affect so many others. When you're not at your best, it impacts how you interact with your team, your peers, and your customers. You are setting the example of what is expected from your employees. If anything, it's expected that you are the one monitoring employees for signs of burnout and making adjustments to ensure an engaged and productive team. Even if you are on the struggle bus, a leader is expected to always show up for others.

When you are an individual contributor or worker bee, you are mostly responsible for yourself. It's about what you own, work-wise, and maybe some team projects. As a leader, this proves even more challenging. You are responsible for everything. There is pressure to meet budgets and operational timelines while making sure your team is engaged and productive. Being a leader is heavily tied to navigating politics, policies, and personalities. In my experience, there was always a push to do more and show up for others, even if it wasn't always in your best interest. Why? Because being a good leader meant putting your teams first—or at least that was the frequent line used to rally the leader troops.

The drumbeat of needing to do more with less. To surpass last year's productivity. To somehow always be upping the ante with the same or fewer resources while keeping your existing team happy. Because if your team isn't happy, it somehow has to be your fault as a leader.

Does any of this sound familiar? Are you feeling burned out just reading that? I might be having a few moments of PTSD just getting this on paper.

Let's take a look at a scenario in which burnout is a component of team dysfunction. Again, read with an open mind and then we'll break it down together.

The Scenario

Marcus is the leader of a high-profile data team within a retail company. This team helps determine the product mix that will be offered in the upcoming season. He currently has four analysts, an incredibly small number for the size of his organization. He has been in this role for two years. In that time, he has had three different direct leaders and was accountable to at least three other senior leaders in the organization due to cross-functional project work. This is primarily due to the company reorganizing to adjust to their own rapid growth and the changing needs of retail. With each reorg, Marcus had to start over in building relationships, educating new leaders on what exactly his team's function was, and managing expectations of new leaders who wanted to do everything their way.

His small but mighty team of four are hard workers. He knows that the workload expected of this team is unrealistic for their size and experience, so he pushes back a great deal and makes every effort to spare his team from knowing all that is swirling outside their purview. His constant goal is to protect them at all costs so they can focus on whatever they have at hand, because mistakes from their team can have million-dollar impacts. Mistakes simply are not an option.

Engagement is important. Marcus knows that keeping his team happy is key to being seen as a good leader. Turnover will only reflect poorly on him. Despite his concern, the employees are as loyal to him as he is to them. They want to protect him from more stress, because they care for him and know the extra-long hours have put a strain on Marcus's family life.

Marcus's newest senior leader, Alicia, is incredibly unforgiving and has added several high-visibility projects to the team's plate. She's often openly dismissive of Marcus in meetings and rarely pays him a compliment even when the work he and his team produce exceeds expectations. She appears to tolerate him because he gets the work done. This is all done in front of Marcus's team, peers, and other leaders in the organization. As a result, Marcus's team has created an "us versus Alicia" mentality.

Marcus begins to confide in the team about his struggles with Alicia in an effort to expose them to more of the reality the team is up against. This only furthers the "ride or die" mentality within the group.

The truth is Marcus is running on fumes. The stress of yet another organizational change and leader, and not having any support from Alicia, is demoralizing as well as soul crushing. He is not sleeping well and has nightmares about work when he does. He also finds his temper is shorter than it should be with everyone around him. He often thinks of looking for another role but is scared of what will happen to his team should he leave. Marcus always chooses to stay for them even though it's costing him personally and, at times, he knows he's not being the leader he hoped to be.

WHAT ARE THE TOXIC BEHAVIORS?

There are many areas to focus on here. Let's start at the very beginning.

- Which parts of this story felt toxic to you?

  _____

  _____

- Who did you think was the most toxic character in this scenario? Why?

  _____

  _____

- What were the most toxic behaviors Marcus exhibited?

  _____

  _____

- Where are there pivot points in this story when Marcus could have made different choices?

  _____

  _____

- What were the toxic behaviors the team exhibited?

  _____

  _____

- What behaviors might Alicia have contributed to a toxic work environment?

  _____

  _____

When reading through this scenario, it might be easy to focus on Marcus, as he is the leader. He clearly is navigating through a lot of organizational challenges, which we know from MIT research mentioned in Chapter 1, is a key indicator of why team members leave organizations. The constant shuffling only adds to the toxic nature of what team members must navigate through, as there is never a settled footing as to what tomorrow may bring.

Let's consider how Marcus is responding to these pressures. What other actions could he take to proactively address his situation? What actions would you want him to take or expect him to take? The reality is, in this scenario, we don't see Marcus asking for help from anyone except his team. As leaders, how and whom we lean on become really important, especially when we are running on fumes. This is where trusted peers and mentors are incredibly important. This means seeking support outside of work, including seeking therapeutic help. Finding those who will provide true perspective and be brutally honest helps keep everyone grounded. This isn't just leadership advice but life advice.

Some will immediately zero in on the constant reorgs and how Alicia is presenting. Not that it isn't an excuse, but is it possible that Alicia is burned out herself? Unless Marcus is willing to talk to her about how her behavior is impacting him and his team, she will continue to be exactly who she is at this moment. Maybe she could use some feedback to reset how she's showing up for those she leads. As I said in the Introduction, we all bring a plate of bullshit to the buffet. Sometimes we need others to help remind us of that.

Regarding the team, this is a perfect example of them completely following the example of their leader. It continues to illustrate the importance of leaders and how their actions set the standard for how the team will respond— and, more importantly, why leaders need to be supported as well.

IMPACT

Let's walk through a few questions to think about how small behaviors create lasting impact.

- What was the impact of Marcus choosing to stay in the role without asking for help?

  _____

  _____

- What was the impact of creating the "ride or die" mentality? For Marcus? For the team? For Alicia?

  _____

  _____

- How did this affect Marcus's ability to effectively lead with clarity and open-mindedness?

  _____

  _____

- How might this dynamic affect his team as they continue to develop professionally within this company?

  _____

  _____

In thinking about the impact, there are multiple aspects to consider. First, let's look at Marcus's team. Marcus's lack of boundaries in the creation of the "us versus them" mentality against Alicia is very unproductive. Even if it would make Marcus feel better for the team to be on his side, so to speak, this definitely is not a winning setup. At the end of the day, Alicia is a leader who has also earned her seat at the table. If her approach is inappropriate, Marcus should have that conversation with her, or at least confer with HR or a mentor to figure out how best to handle it. Creating that hostile wall only furthers a divide, not resolves it.

This behavior may also set the tone for what his team believes is a good leader. Often leaders and subordinates want to be friends, but this is a slippery slope. As leaders, we have to know and set healthy boundaries. In this case, Marcus used his team as a venting tool, which is never okay. As Cy Wakeman points out in *No Ego,* venting tends to lead to more negative thinking and not problem-solving.[7]

The other element we could address is the impact of constant team reorganizations and how these exhaust and fuel a toxic culture. We already know that job instability and reorganizations are top predictors of turnover. This scenario definitely highlights the toll they take, not only on teams, but on leaders as they continue to navigate changing personalities and expectations.

Ultimately, Marcus is on a crash course if he doesn't make some changes. The toxic dynamic between Alicia and him can't continue. His physical health is deteriorating. Eventually, if it hasn't already, his performance will suffer and he will be on the chopping block.

SELF-REFLECTION EXERCISE

Please take a few moments to really think
through the following questions.

- With which person in this scenario did you most
  connect?

  _____

  _____

- What about this person or the scenario most
  resonated with you?

  _____

  _____

- Outside of this scenario, when in the past have
  you been burned out?

  _____

  _____

- How does burnout show up for you? What does it
  look like to others?

  _____

  _____

- Thinking of a past episode in your life, what would you do differently now?

  _____

  _____

- What elements in your environment are most likely to play a role in becoming burned out?

  _____

  _____

- Where could you have set better boundaries today?

  _____

  _____

Gathering Thoughts

Have you been there? Are you there now? We've all seen it. Maybe been there a few times, but often don't realize how far down the path we are until it is too late.

In complete transparency and honesty, I have been here. In moments when I thought I was being a good leader, I can now look back and see that I was completely toast. As a result, I was making decisions that, had I not been so far down a burned road, I would have made differently.

In those moments, I believed I was seeing things clearly and making the right choices. I was putting my team first and getting the work done. I didn't see the actual cost, mostly to myself, until much later. There was so much self-sacrificing that I could have been made a saint. The reality was I was feeding more stress and anxiety into everyone's workday despite my intentions. I was limiting myself and not really setting the example I intended to because I was not setting good boundaries with my team or with my leadership. Simply, I was not leading at that moment.

One of my favorite quotes is from Penny Reid: "Don't set yourself on fire to keep others warm." When I find myself overextending or feeling resentful for putting in more than others are, I remind myself of these words. Being a good leader isn't about giving everything and then giving more. It's about showing up as your best self, which means knowing when and how to say *yes* or *no*. It's about asking for help when you need it from the right people. It is about setting the example by how you show up and actually lead.

CHAPTER 4

Walk the Talk

"What you do speaks so loudly that I cannot hear what you say."

~ Ralph Waldo Emerson

The Setup

I don't know about you, but I love a good leadership quote. Here are some of my favorites:

"Clear is kind."

~ Brené Brown

"A team is not a group of people who work together. A team is a group of people who trust each other."

~ Simon Sinek

"Whether you believe something possible or impossible —either way, you will be right."

~ Cy Wakeman

These words are used to motivate and inspire in moments of doubt, uncertainty, and weakness. We all look at them and probably have a few printed somewhere in our offices. I'd be willing to bet you have your go-to ones when working with your team. Every leader I know has at least one phrase or saying that serves as a guiding principle for them and is frequently shared with their teams and mentees.

Inspirational leaders are labeled so for many reasons. Leaders inspire through their actions. How they show up for their teams is so important. Another way leaders inspire is through their words. It can also be the way they make you feel. If I walk away feeling energized and ready to go, that's usually a good indicator. Good leaders can provide tough feedback to someone and still have them walk away feeling seen, heard, and respected.

Used in the correct context, inspirational words can move mountains. They can help rally the troops when most needed to get the job done. In each case, these events only serve to reinforce the power of the words, their creator, and the leader who wisely deploys them.

Ultimately, good leadership is how all of it (words, actions, feelings) match up. This is where authentic leadership shows up. This is where a leader's actions are thoughtful and intentional. The words are reinforcement of the action and not just the action alone.

Where leaders can fail is when the message does not appear genuine or does not match the overall actions being taken. They're simply words meant to reinforce but not actually connect to the message. For many, it's more of a "do as I say, not as I do" kind of leadership. This can also fall apart when just words replace real leadership. In moments when an employee is looking for true guidance and examples, they are met with quotable quotes and very little actual guidance.

In this scenario, we see an example of how leaning on buzz phrases too heavily and not really leaning into what's happening leaves a team divided and confused.

THE SCENARIO

Penny is the vice president of supply chain and leads a team of about 20 project managers. She's a huge fan of leadership books and has a wall featuring books and motivational sayings from the industry's leaders in professional development. In her organization, she's considered the internal expert for many of the world's top minds in these areas. There isn't a quote from Simon Sinek, Adam Grant, Oprah Winfrey, Brené Brown, or Cy Wakeman she can't whip out at the drop of a hat.

Penny is popular as a mentor. She's highly respected as a supply chain leader within the company and is known for being a walking encyclopedia of inspirational and motivational guidance who has an open-door policy. Anyone on her team, regardless of title, can seek her out for any kind of guidance or support.

Recently, a relatively new supervisor in her team, Curtis, had to provide constructive feedback to an underperforming team member, Bianca. Curtis went to Penny instead of his direct leader, as her door happened to be open and he thought it would be great to just ask her for advice. Because Penny was the more senior leader, he figured her advice would be better than just his direct leader's.

Curtis is nervous, because he is a new people leader and wants help in preparing for the conversation with Bianca. Penny encourages him by saying, in the words of Brené Brown, "Clear is kind." He should be straightforward and concise. Curtis shares his plan with her. Penny likes and approves of Curtis's planned approach and action steps to address Bianca's issues. She wishes him well and encourages him to update her, as she wants to continue to help him grow into being a confident people leader.

Curtis, without talking to his direct leader, proceeds with his feedback conversation with Bianca. Afterward, he feels it went as well as could be expected. However, Bianca is very upset and defensive. Knowing about Penny's open-door policy and feeling she would be sympathetic, Bianca goes straight to Penny's office to complain.

Through tears, Bianca alleges Penny has not been told the whole story and Curtis was accusatory and aggressive. Bianca doesn't agree with his characterization of her performance and feels like it was personal. He just doesn't like her. She doesn't want to work for someone who doesn't value her efforts. She might screw up sometimes, but it isn't that bad. Everyone makes mistakes sometimes, don't they? Bianca says she is thinking of filing a hostile work environment complaint with employee relations against Curtis and Penny. She says they are clearly biased against her for some reason. She might even quit.

Penny calms Bianca and says she will take care of it, telling Bianca no one on her team would be shamed and Curtis's behavior was unacceptable. Penny immediately contacts Curtis and, before he can speak, accuses him of shaming Bianca instead of holding her accountable, as they'd discussed. She expresses disappointment given they had just completed Brené Brown's *Dare to Lead* as part of a leadership book club and had addressed the issue of shaming others. Curtis is very surprised, because he followed her guidance of being clear, concise, and straightforward, making his feedback about the performance and not the person. He thought his approach was what they had agreed upon, especially given he had run it by her first.

Curtis states he did what he thought was right and asks what he could have done differently. Penny responds that she is disappointed in him for not taking responsibility for *his* actions. He, as a leader on her team, has to be willing to accept *his* failure in this situation. If he had truly followed the "Clear is kind" mantra, Bianca wouldn't be upset. Penny suggests he re-read Brené Brown's book because it would help him understand his shortcomings as a leader and how not to shame his employees. She encourages him to lean into his vulnerability at this moment.

Thoroughly bemused, Curtis says he'll do what she is asking but still doesn't understand where he went wrong. Could she provide an example of how he could handle this differently in the future? Penny says to read the book again and then they can discuss his thoughts on where he went wrong and what he believes he can do differently in the future. Curtis walks away scared about how this will affect his role on the team, as well as how this will impact his larger team given that Bianca's poor performance impacts other team members.

WHAT ARE THE TOXIC BEHAVIORS?

All right, time to break this down.

- Which parts of this story felt toxic to you?

  _____

  _____

- Who did you think was the most toxic character in this scenario? Why?

  _____

  _____

- What were the most toxic behaviors exhibited by Penny?

  _____

  _____

- Where are there pivot points in this story when she could have made different choices?

  _____

  _____

- What were the toxic behaviors exhibited by others?

  _____

  _____

A lot is crammed into this scenario, and there are several areas where different choices could have led to a less dramatic outcome. Let's start with the central theme: a leader reinforcing their words with their actions.

In this scenario, Penny is quite skilled with being able to use the right motivational material for those who seek her out. Where the wheels fall off the bus is when her words lack depth. Not being Curtis's direct leader and not being familiar with all the relevant dynamics, she is dipping her toe in and possibly missing the chance to go deeper with Curtis, especially given he is not overly experienced in leading team members. Having a constructive feedback conversation is one of the most challenging tasks for a new leader and simply performing the equivalent of drive-by mentoring is not enough. Although Penny is a tremendous leader in her own right and meant well, she likely isn't as familiar with lower-level team issues. The reality is living her own mantra to be clear would have been to coach Curtis to seek support from his direct leader or from his human resources business partner in the lead-up to his conversation with Bianca.

It is also very clear that Penny heavily leans on Brené Brown's "Clear is kind" as a leadership expectation but fails to live up to those words with her own actions. There is no clarity or kindness for Curtis at the end of this scenario. He is seeking real leadership in this moment and is met with words with little actual meaning. She is holding him to a behavioral standard that she is not living up to herself.

Some might argue the open-door policy is a problem, but I'd challenge to say the structure of its use might be a toxic element, especially if it gives team members this permission to skip their actual leadership chain to complain or get advice. Equally, Penny should have offered an open ear to both Curtis and Bianca but not immediately jumped to conclusions. This would have been a good opportunity to coach them, direct them to the right leader for next steps, and not become part of the drama. (We get into open-door policies more in the next section.)

Lastly, I want to focus on Bianca. We don't have a lot of specifics, but what we do know is she feels upset and is threatening the leader and the organization unless she gets what she wants. I don't know many people who love getting constructive feedback, and I feel pretty certain most leaders have had some employees push back during these conversations. What's important is how it's handled. In this case, Penny leaves Curtis with little actionable guidance as to next steps. Clear would, indeed, be kind in this moment.

IMPACT

Let's walk through a few questions to think about how small behaviors create lasting impact.

- How important is it for a leader to practice what they preach?

  _____

  _____

- What was the impact of Penny's open-door policy?

  _____

  _____

- What was the impact of Penny's response to the Curtis and Bianca feedback session?

  _____

  _____

- What was the impact on Curtis when Penny told him to read a book versus talking him through the situation?

  _____

  _____

- What could be the impact on the team if Curtis doesn't hold Bianca accountable?

  _____

  _____

Let's talk about Penny's leveraging of a leadership book in this learning moment. I don't know about you, but I've shelves full of leadership books from throughout the years. I've had leaders use them as book clubs and some for training. Many provided great insights I have leveraged throughout my career, and many are simply collecting dust.

Penny should embrace her role and demonstrate the teachings versus just pointing to the book. The impact here feels more like a "do as I say, not as I do" vibe. Brené

Brown is brilliant. Her words are incredibly powerful. However, they would be much more powerful if Penny internalized them and led by example. Her actions in this scenario are not kind. Not kind to Curtis, nor to his direct leader (who is completely in the dark), nor to Bianca.

I want to talk about how, when executed well, an open-door policy can be a game-changer for teams. It serves as a means to communicate, engage, and generally get to know all levels of employees along the power spectrum. Throughout my career, I've seen various leaders use an open-door policy as a means to encourage engagement and the sense of community. It's also wonderful to allow for interactions across different employee and leader levels within a division and not just direct reports.

This example, however, highlights a way this policy can go wrong or be used in a misguided way. Using the open-door policy to bypass an actual leadership chain, versus using it as a sounding board or "get to know you" moment, is where things can go wrong. In this example, it shows how mistrust across leadership levels can result from lack of communication among leaders who should be in-the-know. You could also argue it creates complexity in holding team members accountable when the chain of command is not involved.

Erosion of trust is definitely a factor in team member engagement and, ultimately, turnover. This includes the leaders within Penny's team, as well as individual contributors. People need structure and they need to know what to depend on. If words are meaningless or if it's easy to circumvent your leader to get what you want, drama will ensue. This is not a culture for a successful team.

SELF-REFLECTION EXERCISE

Please take a few moments to really think
through the following questions.

- What part of this story felt toxic to you?

  _____

  _____

- What about this person or the scenario most
  resonated with you?

  _____

  _____

- Have you had moments when you gave guidance
  that you were not or would not follow yourself?

  _____

  _____

- What would you do differently now?

  _____

  _____

- Outside of this scenario, when have you found
  yourself frustrated with a subordinate because of
  you not clearly communicating your position?

  _____

  _____

- When have you found yourself stumped over feedback you have received from a leader? And walked away feeling lost and confused?

_____

_____

Gathering Thoughts

People in leadership positions often get there because they are good at getting things done and solving problems. At times, we all want to jump into solution mode versus leading and coaching those we lead. In being a good leader, it is important to always reflect on what we are doing and saying versus the impact. For instance, think about how what we are saying is helping or hurting a situation. Slowing down, as a leader, can be hard, but we must, especially when providing guidance.

Open-door policies aren't inherently a bad thing. It is all in how a leader structures them and uses them to model the behavior they would like to see. For example, an impromptu drop-in is a great opportunity to be curious, ask probing questions, and allow your team to discover the right path forward. It doesn't necessarily require you to be the solution, which is where you might naturally want to gravitate. We are meant to lead, not simply direct.

We all know the importance of words—the words that are spoken and, more importantly, the words that are left unsaid. As a leader, it is so important to never underestimate the impact of our communication. One of my favorite quotes from Brené Brown's book *The Gifts of Imperfection* is "Authenticity is a collection of choices that we have to make every day. It's about the choice to show up and be real. The choice to let our true selves be seen."[8] Using others' words to motivate and lead isn't the problem. The issue is when we, as leaders, don't use them in the context we should or do not actually practice what we are preaching.

When leaning too heavily on the work of others and not simply integrating our own leadership experiences, leaders can come across as lacking authenticity and vulnerability. What matters is how to implement concepts and thoughts in a realistic, humanistic way.

When leaders use others' words and works, when timed correctly, they can serve to truly connect and energize a team member or a whole group. I have carried this lesson into how I lead teams. It was a way to bring the human, including levity and humor, to a group, allowing for the message to sink in, to appear genuine in how I was communicating and the meaningful information I wanted them to receive. But catchy phrases can never serve as a replacement for actual leadership.

In my closing thoughts, a quote from Christine Kane comes to mind: "Consistent action results in consistent results."[9] When most read it, they see it through the most positive of connotations. Consistent hard work results in consistent good results. Right? Well, consistent action—even poor action or misdirection—will consistently produce the same results too. Consistently not holding someone accountable will result in that person consistently underperforming. Anything you do consistently will produce the outcomes reflecting the initiating action. Taking some moments to reflect on your approaches and how they actually show up in your leadership is absolutely critical.

CHAPTER 5

Fear and Loathing in the Office

"In a closed society where everybody's guilty,
the only crime is getting caught. In a world of
thieves, the only final sin is stupidity."

~ Hunter S. Thompson

The Setup

Let's start with an obvious truth about conflict. I've yet to meet a leader who loves conflict, unless they're somewhat of a sociopath. Most people I know address it because they have to as part of being a leader, but they don't really seek it out. Because of the collective hesitation in tackling conflict, they often approach it from a half-hearted perspective or end up softening their initial approach because they don't want to upset or make people mad. I don't need stats to back this up. If you're like me, you have a list of names scrolling through your mind of great leaders who have fallen prey to this.

For new leaders, it gets even more challenging, as new leaders are a fun mix of confidence, fear, and limited experience. They have this new, fancy title that instills the confidence they've earned this leader role but also are now responsible for taking on some very difficult conversations to have a functional and productive team. I have seen people, given their limited experience, be so fearful they avoid conflict as much as possible, resulting in a disgruntled and disengaged team. Or worse, they race in with no fear and make demands, moving people into a confrontational place. Both approaches leave a lot to be desired and often do not yield the intended results.

One area that's often a challenge for leaders to address is poor performance. This is especially true when talking about employees who are typically well liked. However, recent research shows employees are more likely to leave companies that fail to distinguish between high performers and slackers when it comes to recognition and rewards.[10] In other words, tolerating poor performers creates an inequity. Leaders are sending the message that actual work doesn't matter as long as you have some other redeeming qualities. Or, the leader is too scared or not supported enough to address the issue. Either way, this is a breeding ground for toxicity and turnover.

Even in companies with overall good cultures, there can be pockets when there's a hesitation or an unwillingness to address issues because of fear of conflict. Over my career, I've seen every leader, including great ones, falter in embracing the inherent conflict that often arises from holding individuals accountable. I've said it before and will say it frequently: Being a leader is hard. It isn't meant for everyone, but if you find yourself in the role, you have got to learn how to step up or step aside. Your teams deserve it, especially your top performers.

Let's take a look at a new people leader who has some big decisions to make.

The Scenario

John was recently hired as a new leader of a nonprofit organization. He's never been a people leader before, despite having had prior leadership roles, and is really nervous, but he is super excited because he's worked hard to earn the experience to be seen as a well-rounded leader. In this new role, he will be leading a team of veteran employees. Many have been with the organization for more than 20 years.

Based on some great advice from one of his mentors, John has taken his time to get to know the team and get his feet under him with regard to what his role really is and where there are gaps in the business. After six months of holding team and individual meetings, he feels he has a good grasp on each person and their performance, and now feels ready to start making some important changes, including one that may cause some resistance.

The biggest change is related to Brenda. She's been around for more than two decades and is loved by almost everyone. She's seen as the "mom" of the office and is married to the former director. She is also close friends with some people on the board of directors. She's often one of the first people to volunteer to help when it's needed and is often seen as the funniest person in the office, often bringing an element of laughter everywhere she goes.

The problem is she doesn't actually do her job. She rarely works a full day and generally shows up and leaves whenever it's convenient for her. There have also been times when supplies she's responsible for maintaining have been unaccounted for. One time, her personal charges ended up on the nonprofit credit card. Through an indirect and more friend-like approach, John has so far suggested improvements with little success.

To be honest, Brenda actually scares John a bit. Any other person would've been fired a long time ago, but some of the team just works around her and, generally, is apologetic about her faults as "it's just Brenda." The overwhelming attitude is she's just forgetful or it was just an accident. Brenda also frequently leans on her peers to help her out when she's just "forgetful" or has simply not done her work because of a sudden "personal crisis," often rewarding them with treats and little gifts. When they don't, she spreads gossip that they are not team players. Overall, her faults and lack of performance have just been accepted throughout the years.

As mentioned, Brenda has a big personality. When she walks in the room, a lot of people (including John) are drawn to her sense of humor. However, this isn't true for every member of the team. About half of the team really struggle with the lack of accountability and wish she were gone. They've been very vocal with John in private meetings, saying they are tired of picking up her slack and being accused of not being team players simply because they won't fix her messes. They want change: Either get Brenda to do her job or get someone who will.

John knows he can't let this behavior continue. Part of the reason he was brought in was to bring new life into the business. Brenda is not in support of John's proposed changes and, at times, is openly hostile to changing anything about how the nonprofit operates.

John can't afford to have half of his team quit, which they will likely do if he doesn't get this situation under control. But he is scared to upset Brenda, as she has so much influence with some board members and the part of the team that loves her.

The reality is John can't just do nothing, which is what he's been doing. One morning, after giving himself a pep talk and an extra shot of espresso, John calls Brenda in, determined to hold her accountable. Fired up on caffeine, he launches into a laundry list of where Brenda is just not meeting expectations. He tells her she needs to change her ways immediately or she's going to be fired. Brenda squares her shoulders and defiantly demands proof of every allegation. She begins to cry and says John simply doesn't like her and that's the real issue. John just doesn't like having an older person on the staff and the board wouldn't like a discrimination complaint.

John, in a panic, backpedals and softens his stance. He wasn't expecting Brenda to start crying. I mean, why is she crying? John immediately apologizes for upsetting her and says they'll need to work through it together. There's no need to be alarmed or alert the board. Brenda asks to be excused, as she's simply too upset to work for the rest of the day. John, fearing what she'll do if he doesn't say yes, gives Brenda the rest of the day off.

After a flurry of tears and tissues, Brenda calmly leaves John's office. Weaving her way around the cubes, she smiles as she tells everyone John has given her the day off and they'll need to cover her work for the day. Once she finally leaves, John sits in his office a bit dumbfounded over where he went wrong and what he should do next.

WHAT ARE THE TOXIC BEHAVIORS?

- Which parts of this story felt toxic to you?

  _____

  _____

- Who did you think was the most toxic character in this scenario? Why?

  _____

  _____

- What were the most toxic behaviors exhibited by John?

  _____

  _____

- Where are there pivot points in this story when she could have made different choices?

  _____

  _____

- What were the toxic behaviors exhibited by the team?

  _____

  _____

When looking at this scenario, most people focus on the historical trend of Brenda being allowed to behave in the manner she has for such an extended period. I encourage you to consider the enablers. Those include her peers and the board members. They, too, have a responsibility to hold each other accountable—even people they like or love to be around. This would also include her husband, given she would have been employed under his leadership (although I imagine that would have made home life difficult and is among the reason there are rules against nepotism in most businesses).

John has taken the step to get to really know his team before introducing any change. This is a great best practice as a new leader because too much change too soon or the wrong change can add to the confusion and toxic nature of what's going on within a team. When he finally confronts Brenda and her behavior, he backs down quickly when faced with resistance and tears. This is not uncommon for new leaders. It can be unsettling to see someone become emotional and angry, specifically when it's directed at you.

For many, the natural tendency will be to "fix" it or to try to soften the approach to lessen the blow. In this case, I'd have encouraged him to leverage his mentor and more experienced peers more, especially in the lead-up to confronting Brenda. It's never easy to approach these conversations (particularly if you're new to these kinds of situations), but they do become easier when you're prepared with what you want to say, how you're going to say it, and expected outcomes.

Ultimately, he needs to fully step into his role and embrace the conflict that will come with creating a more accountable culture within this group.

IMPACT

Let's walk through a few questions to think about how small behaviors create lasting impact.

- What is the impact if John does nothing to address the accountability culture within his team?

　　_____

　　_____

- Is it possible for John to salvage Brenda as an employee? If yes, how should he approach that situation? What would the impact be?

　　_____

　　_____

The reality is John must do something, because the impact of doing nothing results in massive turnover and, ultimately, he'll not be a leader for long. The board will not have confidence in him. The safest and smartest place to start is to introduce a culture of accountability for everyone, explaining his expectations and consequences when they're not met. This creates a level playing field for everyone. He needs to be compassionate and consistent, as change is not linear or easy for most people.

Holding people accountable isn't easy. You get labeled as being mean and unfair when the truth is you have to create an environment that's equal and fair for everyone. Cy Wakeman describes one of the best approaches to creating a culture of accountability in her book *Reality-Based Leadership*. Employees are given two options: to create a plan to perform the role as expected or to create a transition plan off of the team. There is no third option. You, as a leader, are there to support their chosen plan, but it's up to the employee to make a choice and then create their plan.[11] It puts the power in the employee's hands while allowing the leader to have standards. The key here is kindness comes from consistency. They should always know what to expect from you.

John will also need the board's support and should include them in his plan for moving the nonprofit forward and what that will mean for the team. Given the personal history here with Brenda, he'll need to leverage as much support as he can. He'll also need to show an overall approach, not just one for Brenda. This isn't just about her. It is about creating a fair and equitable culture across the team.

This doesn't mean all will be easy-peasy, but it sets the stage for John to have the difficult conversations when employees are not meeting expectations. And who knows, Brenda could step up once this new culture is in place and others might struggle. You simply don't know until you try and create consistency.

SELF-REFLECTION EXERCISE

Please take a few moments to really think
through the following questions.

- With which person in this scenario did you most
connect?

_____

_____

- What about this person or the scenario most
resonated with you?

_____

_____

- When have you allowed fear to control your
decision-making as a leader?

_____

_____

- What elements in your environment played a role
in your fear of doing the right thing?

_____

_____

- Where could you have asked for help or sought more support?

  _____

  _____

- Considering this past experience, what would you do differently now?

  _____

  _____

Gathering Thoughts

As a new leader, there's a lot of pressure and imposter syndrome. I was often scared to do the wrong thing when I was starting out and, heaven forbid, piss off the wrong people. Truth is, it happened. I didn't die from it. I didn't get fired. What I did was learn a lot and try each time to be better than I was before.

One truth I have come to appreciate is, if you are doing your job right, everyone will not be happy all the time with you. To say you are a leader of a team in which everyone is completely happy all the time is not being honest or aware of what your team really feels. Leaders are human and need to set realistic expectations for us and those around us. This doesn't mean I have an unengaged group. It just means there will be times when I won't do or say things to please every single person. Guess what? That's okay and is a true part of being a leader.

As I gained experience, I learned how to embrace fear

and lead at the same time. Notice the fear is still there. It's okay to say there are scary moments as a leader. Don't let anyone fool you. Everyone has something that causes moments of questioning and doubt. What makes a good leader is the ability to acknowledge it and keep going. As Ralph Waldo Emerson said, "Fear defeats more people than any other one thing in the world."

Let's not be defeated.

CHAPTER 6

I'm Pretty Sure I Am God

The universe is God.
I am God so that means I am the universe.

~ Oscar Wilde

The Setup

With all the various kinds of leaders that exist in the world, it's hard not to have interacted with at least one who behaved as if they had not been hand-selected by God to be a leader, if not an actual god or a goddess themselves. As we discussed in the beginning of the book, there are leaders who possess personality traits and not just behaviors. This chapter gets into those characteristics that are more of a narcissistic nature. It's all about the leader who really focuses on how awesome they are, often at the expense of those around them.

This is not to diminish the notion that many narcissistic leaders are high performers and get things done. Think of people like Steve Jobs and Jeff Bezos. Many leaders are absolute visionaries and are sought out for their expertise. Many senior executives get to where they are because they're incredibly confident in themselves, and this confidence has not led them astray. They get things done or they know how to get others to get things done. They can be absolutely magnetic as a result of their belief, vision, and ability to attain whatever goal they seek. But let's be honest for a second: Narcissists can also be incredibly difficult to work with—or, as most who work with or for them might say, they are brilliant assholes.

Many have developed this belief they are the smartest people in the room and can manipulate any situation. However great narcissistic leaders can be, there can be—and usually is—a dark side. Confidence can tip into arrogance and unchecked ego, leaving those who follow them feeling drained, unseen, and unappreciated.

We know through the MIT research mentioned throughout the book there's higher turnover when high performers don't feel recognized and rewarded for their work, but they also found higher turnover of highly innovative workplaces like Tesla because work/life balance and manageable workloads are nonexistent.[12] Again, leaders who create these environments can be brilliant, but they can also be in their own world and not concerned about those surrounding them. This leads to a challenging environment for employees, who have to be comfortable working within their limits and living in the shadow of their greatness.

Let's take a look at a scenario in which a leader is operating from a place of ego and arrogance.

THE SCENARIO

Abigail has just taken a lateral move as a new leader and reports to Peter, a senior leader in the branding department. Despite being the only female leader on the team, she is excited to work for someone so respected for getting things done and being a great strategic mind. Her early observations include that Peter can be a bit short with everyone, particularly behind closed doors. He has very high expectations of those who report to him and little patience when those expectations aren't met.

During her first few weeks, Abigail asks for feedback on her performance thus far. Peter's initial comment is that she really has some areas she needs to improve on to stay on his team. For example, she doesn't speak up enough. She needs to try harder to share her thoughts on strategy, because he needs to see what kind of brain she actually has. Ultimately, Peter knows when someone is going to be a star, and he's not sure about her.

Abigail thanks him for the feedback and promises to do better. After getting his feedback, she really tries to share thoughts when it seems appropriate. She sometimes finds it hard on a male-dominated team to get in any words. On one occasion, during a strategy brainstorm, she is asked to go grab coffee for the team before the meeting starts. Peter is adamant she "get it right" because most women "screw it up" so he demands she write down everyone's order. He wants his coffee to be like he likes it: with just enough milk so it looks like Beyoncé. The rest of the team give her their orders and quickly go back to work as she departs for the closest coffee shop.

Given that Abigail feels more like an intern and less like a leader on the team, she decides to reach out to one of her peers, Chad, to get some insight and advice. He has been on the team for five years and appears to have a good handle on how to manage up with Peter.

Chad is very open with her and applauds her tenacity in trying to get seen on such a competitive team. He says she just needs to figure out how to outdo her peers, even if it means being underhanded. He lets her know that Peter values those who succeed at all costs, and she needs to have really thick skin to withstand his constant criticisms. He also tells her, even if Peter likes an idea, she'd never get real credit for it. Peter always takes credit for anything that comes from the team. What she should value is all the great things she can learn from being around him (essentially, play the game) and try to leverage her connections and learnings to get her next role somewhere else (because she will never get promoted above the others on the team).

After getting all of this from Chad and constantly trying new things to no avail, Abigail feels exhausted. She is tired of trying to speak up in an effort to gain Peter's attention and approval, only to be talked over by her peers. All her ideas are quickly dismissed by Peter, who claims they aren't strategic or visionary enough. She feels defeated and that maybe she is just not approaching her role in the right way. After engaging several external mentors for guidance, Abigail decides (a bit nervously) to try a new approach with Peter: to seek his insight around something she is working on. This would allow her to gain more access to how he views things and generate discussion on her thoughts as well.

In her regularly scheduled one-on-one, while providing him her update, Abigail asks a clarifying question regarding a regional strategy. Peter immediately sits back in his chair, flares his nostrils, and appears angry. A bit fearful, she asks if there was something wrong. Peter curtly informs her she isn't good enough. Any good strategic leader would not need to ask clarifying questions, and she is clearly not a strategic thinker. Raising his hand above his head, Peter says, "I'm up here," and then drops his hand close to the floor and finishes with "You're down here." He had had high hopes for her, but she just isn't cutting it. She isn't strategic enough to be on his team, and it isn't a skill he is confident she could learn. Without a comment from Abigail, Peter says he'll talk to HR about a transition elsewhere in the company because he'd hate to have to fire her.

WHAT ARE THE TOXIC BEHAVIORS?

- Which parts of this story felt toxic to you?

  _____

  _____

- Who did you think was the most toxic character in this scenario? Why?

  _____

  _____

- What were the most toxic behaviors exhibited by Peter?

  _____

  _____

- How are the team dynamics toxic?

  _____

  _____

Let's start with Peter. His misogynistic and subtly racist comments definitely create a challenging and toxic environment. As the most senior leader, Peter sets the tone and the example for those who report up to him. His ego creates a situation in which he doesn't recognize the team effort in creating success and only attributes it to himself.

Sadly, the culture Peter creates is reflected in Chad's insights into the backstabbing that goes on. Speaking from personal experience, when you're unable to trust those around you, it's crippling. High performers don't stay for long on teams in which they never know who they can trust. Eventually they gain whatever they can and move on to a less-volatile team or work environment.

IMPACT

Let's walk through a few questions to think about how small behaviors create lasting impact.

- **What is the healthiest next step for Abigail?**

  _____

  _____

- **What is the long-term impact of Abigail's experience on this team?**

  _____

  _____

- **What is the impact of Peter's leadership style?**

  _____

  _____

- **What is the cascading impact on the rest of the team?**

  _____

  _____

When reflecting on this scenario and leaders like Peter, the impacts can be very long lasting. I've been drawn to and worked with many Peters throughout the years. When you're successful and make them look good, life is sweet, even if you're living in a bit of a shadow. Influential leaders like Peter are seen as credible, and their opinions carry weight. They can make or break careers and reputations, so the impact of working with or for a Peter-like leader can be life-changing.

In this scenario, the impact of Peter's behaviors is the reinforcement of the status quo being what is valued to him. Peter likes being #1 and creating a team where cut-throat competition is the name of the game. Also, the male peer leaders are being reinforced that Peter's style of leadership is acceptable, if not outright rewarded.

It would be understandable for Abigail to have some confidence issues given her experience and dismissal from the team. Depending on his comments to others within the organization, Peter has immense power and influence in where she goes next and how those leaders will perceive her.

SELF-REFLECTION EXERCISE

Please take a few moments to really think through the following questions.

- With which person did you most resonate?

  _____

  _____

- When have you dismissed an employee's contributions out of hand?

  _____

  _____

- What elements exist in your leadership style that might be narcissistic in nature?

  _____

  _____

- When have you been dismissed and felt disrespected by your leader?

  _____

  _____

- How are you creating a safe space for your team to share thoughts, receive constructive feedback, and grow professionally?

  _____

  _____

Gathering Thoughts

While writing this chapter, I frequently thought about this Cy Wakeman quote: "In the workplace, the differences between confidence and ego can make or break your career."[13] The reality has been that leaders, no matter how toxic, have been rewarded in the past as long as they got results. Although gains are being made in addressing these kinds of leaders, we still have a way to go.

There will always be leaders who create cultures of fear, favoritism, and competition. The reality is this approach is not about creating well-rounded leaders or sustainable teams. Team members may learn something, but eventually they move on because it's exhausting to constantly be looking over your shoulder. The challenge for companies is, despite the negatives, being honest about how they reward toxic leadership, even if unintentionally.

This becomes really important, because one leader can infect a whole company. Many leaders take on the styles of those they report to. At times, this is because they're good traits or behaviors you would want to emulate. At others, it's a matter of survival. You become who you think you need to be in order to simply survive or until you can find another role. When a company keeps a toxic leader like Peter, it creates the crack for more people to emulate his style and slowly erode a healthy culture. We all simply have to do better and be better for our teams.

CHAPTER 7

Where My Single People At?

*"Just because I'm single, it doesn't mean I'm alone.
I have food and internet."*

~ Anonymous

The Setup

I don't know about you, but I don't necessarily think of my peers and coworkers as family. Yes, we spend a lot of time together, and some become incredibly close friends, but that doesn't mean I'd be willing to share my deepest, darkest secrets with all of them. Hell, when I was going through my divorce, I only told three coworkers. (I didn't want them to be concerned when I had to take off suddenly for attorney calls and therapy sessions.) Why? Because it wasn't really anyone's business. Why would it matter as long as I was meeting my performance goals?

Why am I sharing this? Because what we choose to share with our leaders and teams can and does matter, regardless whether it should. This chapter is about how unconscious biases play out specifically around marital status and family status. In a perfect world, it wouldn't or shouldn't but, alas, here we are.

Like some of my peers, I have experienced a bit of discrimination due to my child-free and single status. Ultimately, some leaders make important delegation and promotional decisions based on factors like marital status, parental status, and assumed household income. I have a feeling this chapter will touch a nerve for most people, and I ask that you read it through before going on to the next chapter or stop reading the book altogether.

If you think I'm crazy or being overly sensitive, research indicates I'm (reasonably) sane. Bella DePaulo, a Harvard PhD researcher, published a book investigating the single person's experience in the workplace titled *Singled Out*. DePaulo has even gone so far as to coin the term *Singlism,* which represents the treatment of single persons or the unattached.[14] Essentially, her work has shown workplaces perpetuate the belief that plays into the worst stereotypes of single people: They don't have a life. Or worse, their life matters less than that of a married or committed person.

As a single person, I'm often amazed by the immediate assumptions people make about my personal life. For instance, some people are pretty open about their belief that single, child-free employees can and, more importantly, should take on more because they have less responsibility at home or, worse, they aren't in need of financial growth in the same way because they only have their own expenses to worry about. DePaulo's work not only validates this but finds this financial assumption was alive and well across employers. Essentially, employers assume a singleton's home life is less financially strained than that of a married peer.

It all comes down to the assumptions that single people have no lives simply because they aren't married—when the reality is people typically only share certain parts of their lives at work. Just because someone is single does not mean they don't have familial responsibilities or they aren't heavily involved in something that is just as consuming as anyone else's circumstances.

Now before all my married folks with their beautiful children start cursing me out and slamming this book shut, I think it's important to call out many of my peers who have commented on the workplace challenges of having a family. They're subjected to equally unfair assumptions that they don't or can't work as hard as their child-free and single peers. They feel unfairly judged when they do need flexibility to take care of family needs. Know that I see and hear you even if the scenario in this chapter is focused on those in a different life circumstance.

As much as many companies want their teams to "feel like a family," this simply isn't the reality for many. When faced with a team you don't necessarily trust, why would anyone divulge all their personal information? Although this chapter title and scenario examine the prejudice against single women, I've seen similar attitudes apply to single men. Basically, it boils down to "You can take on more projects or work longer hours because you don't have anyone depending on you after work." Let's examine how this has played out in the workplace.

THE SCENARIO

Cheryl is the leader of a very productive team that is close-knit and engaged. It's a diverse group filled with different genders, ages, and familial statuses. In a recent surge of high-profile and time-intensive projects, Cheryl reaches out to two employees to notify them they have been assigned some new projects. These new assignments come because their backgrounds are well suited to work needed and also because they don't have kids to worry about. She feels they'll do a great job and it will just be easier for them to work the longer hours without sacrificing family life.

The two team members are happy to help, however are uncomfortable being given such an intense workload, in part because Cheryl thinks they have more time. Child-free Jenny is single and working toward her MBA at night. She hasn't shared this with anyone at work for fear people might think she is a flight risk. Child-free Samuel, on the other hand, is very newly married and still trying to adjust to this life change.

In an effort to not make waves, they both vent to each other but put their heads down and knock the work out of the park. This is what good team players do, they say. Great teams show up and help each other out.

All is good until an in-team promotion becomes available. After getting down to the final two candidates, Jenny and another team member, David, Cheryl calls Jenny into her office to discuss the final decision. Cheryl tells Jenny the role is going to David. When Jenny asks what she could do differently to improve her chances in the future, Cheryl informs her she is a perfect candidate for future consideration, especially once she shared she was pursuing her MBA. She's told to keep doing what she's doing. When it came down to it, the only major difference was David really needs the extra income since he is the breadwinner for his family and Jenny, given her child-free status, isn't in as great of a need for a higher salary.

Jenny is stunned by this insight and really upset, given she has gone above and beyond whenever asked. Also, David doesn't have an MBA, nor is he planning to get one. This feels more like a slap in the face and makes Jenny resentful. It also leaves her reconsidering if this is the right place for her to be professionally.

WHAT ARE THE TOXIC BEHAVIORS?

- What did you feel were the most toxic behaviors?

  _____

  _____

- What made them toxic to you?

  _____

  _____

- What are toxic behaviors demonstrated by Cheryl?

  _____

  _____

- What cultural elements support a toxic organizational environment?

  _____

  _____

- What assumptions did you make in this scenario?

  _____

  _____

When considering this scenario, let's look at Cheryl first. Her leadership style is clearly one based on desired transparency, even if it's not appropriate and she misses the mark. Her decision to assign Jenny and Samuel to take on the sudden workload increase is, in part, based on skill set. From that standpoint, things are good, but it all takes a turn when she also includes her assumption or bias that they have more time since they don't have children.

The better way to approach this would be to consider the skill sets needed and then talk to those employees. To avoid making assumptions, Cheryl could ask the team who wants to take on this responsibility. If she just needs to make a decision quickly, Cheryl should use her team members' skill sets and professional capacity as her guide, not make assumptions based on people's personal lives.

The other element many have seen play out (I know I have) is creating financial work opportunities based on non-performance-related factors. Giving David the promotion even in part because he is the breadwinner for his family makes for a challenging precedent. What Cheryl is communicating is when all is equal at work your personal life becomes the deciding factor. Discrimination can come into play. Why? Because you never know what is really happening in someone's personal life. We make decisions largely based on what we think we know. And we already know that's mostly likely not right.

Promotions should be based solely on work performance and skill set, not assumptions about anyone's personal bank account. Now, I can hear some of you saying, "If you know David is struggling financially, this promotion could be a retention effort, given all else is the same." As a leader, you wouldn't want to lose him to a higher-paying role with another organization. This is fair. Especially in light of the Great Resignation, people will leave your team if they get a better offer.

Let's look at this issue a bit more.

IMPACT

Let's walk through a few questions to think about how small behaviors create lasting impact.

- What was the impact of Cheryl's assumptions when assigning work?

  _____

  _____

- How will this impact the team's engagement?

  _____

  _____

- What is the possible impact of giving a promotion based on personal life assumptions and not work performance?

  _____

  _____

Let's start with how Cheryl delegates work and the assumptions she makes about everyone's capacity. Choosing Jenny and Samuel because they don't have children could create resentment not only against Cheryl for her assumptions, but for team members who did not get the heavier workload. There is already evidence this one action resulted in these employees venting to each other, creating a slippery slope of an "us versus them" dynamic. For a team that seems to work fairly well together, making such significant assumptions will cause cracks to develop as decisions are clearly being made based on something other than fairness and actual performance. In situations like this, it is important to be mindful of what brings the team together and to be transparent while also being fair.

In the Introduction we discussed that employees leave cultures where true work is rewarded the same as subpar efforts. Jenny took on an assignment, killed it, and was passed over for basically not having a family. Why would she stay somewhere that created such an unlevel experience and did not appear to value her efforts? Seriously, why would Jenny choose to stay? With everything being equal, if a leader were worried about losing David, should they not worry about losing Jenny too?

No one wants to be viewed through a biased lens. They

want to be respected and rewarded for hard and good work.

SELF-REFLECTION EXERCISE

Please take a few moments to really think through the following questions.

- With which person did you most resonate?

  _____

  _____

- What about their situation was familiar to you?

  _____

  _____

- When have you judged someone else based on what you knew (or thought you knew) about their personal situation (e.g., "I need this bonus more than she does because I have kids to support")?

  _____

  _____

- When have you felt your behavior judged for your personal relationship or familial status?

  _____

  _____

- What biases do you have that you might need to change?

  _____

  _____

Gathering Thoughts

As the old saying goes, don't assume, because it makes an ass out of you and me. Single and child-free employees deserve better than baseless assumptions. To simply assume these statuses mean you lead a more isolated, unfulfilled life is (excuse my language) bullshit.

I've seen good-intentioned leaders fall into this trap. I've been guilty of this. I've caught myself saying things like "Thomas has a two-income household so he doesn't need a promotion. Jackie is on her own and really needs the money more." Again, this is wrong and I'm not judging anyone for falling into this hole. The important part is to be aware of it if these words fall from your lips or the thoughts float through your head.

Assumptions create a breeding ground for a toxic work environment, one that pits people against each other. Quite simply, it shouldn't be this way. This is lazy leadership and a means to pander. It would be better to ask people who wants to take on more responsibility rather than to make assumptions. Just because someone is single doesn't mean they might not have other responsibilities the office is not aware of—nor might it be their business to know. Unlike what many companies proclaim, we are not family, and I, as an employee, do not (nor should I) have to tell you all of my personal life story to be treated fairly in the workplace.

Whether you are in a relationship or whether you have kids shouldn't be factor into how work is assigned or how promotions are handed out. When considering who can take on more work or who needs to make more money, the decision needs to be based on actual performance and fairness. It's fine to ask who might be willing to step up to take on a heavier project. It is not fine to just assume.

CHAPTER 8

You've Got a Friend in Me

"What's most important in a friendship?
Tolerance and loyalty."

~ J.K. Rowling

The Setup

As a people leader, I have to make a pretty big confession. We all have people we prefer to be around. Yes, I have had favorites. Like most leaders (and, let's be honest, parents), there is always one you just like a little more than the others. It could be because of personality, life circumstances, time working together, or whatever it is that draws people together. I've had some employees who were and are still some of my favorite people, and many have become my friends.

In my case, the favored were high-performing workers

who showed up, got work done, and created a nice team environment. Not a lot of drama to get it done, either. Through my lens, they were the best of the best. I did my best to ensure these employees were engaged, and I made sure they knew I was as loyal to them as they were to me by rewarding them with recognition. If we're still being honest, their peers might have considered these employees suck-ups and brown-nosers.

It's important to point out that favoring someone isn't inherently bad. Cy Wakeman challenged conventional logic with her thoughts on having favorites in what she termed *working with the willing*.[15] Wakeman believes having favorites is good as long as it's tied to accountability and performance. People who get things done should be rewarded with recognition and attention. Conversely, people who just complain and aren't showing up to get it done should *not* be rewarded with a lot of attention and definitely should not be favorites, despite them having a great sense of humor or other redeeming quality. Note Wakeman's version of favoritism is *not* tied to an unconscious bias related to gender, race, political affiliation, and so forth. It's tied specifically to people who are prone to accountable action—those who get on board with whatever leadership is asking them to do.

Leaders being unable to separate their employees' likeability from their actual work performance is where things go off the rails. It's when, as a leader, you don't hold team members equally accountable for the same behavior, or you treat them differently than you would another employee simply because you like them more. Again, this is likely where unconscious bias sneaks in. It's also where employees can use their known favorability to get unequal and preferential treatment.

We have all seen leaders who have different expectations of people in similar roles, or how some team members never seem to face consequences throughout our careers. Hell, we *are* some of those people! Let's be honest. Most of us have likely benefited from being favored, including promotions or better project assignments. Or maybe a time when a less-than-stellar performance was allowed to slide simply because your leader knew you could do better and gave you the benefit of the doubt this one (or one more) time.

We all have seen the downside of this slippery slope, including being overlooked for recognition or work assignments. Or maybe in uneven performance expectations and evaluations. When the favored are given more leeway or latitude than the unfavored because "I know them" and "It just doesn't sound like them." When your feet were held a little closer to the fire than someone else's.

Realizing we've all seen it and, honestly, have done it ourselves, leads to an important question: Does this make us a bad leader? Maybe. Maybe not. The answer depends on intentionality and awareness. It definitely feels and is terrible to those treated unfairly, and this is never okay. How do I know? I have been the less-favored employee too. We all have at some point in our careers. It sucks to feel unseen and, more importantly, to feel as if my perspective or thoughts were dismissed simply because I wasn't "vibing" with or better liked by my leader—again, having nothing to do with whether I was doing a good job.

Let's look at a scenario in which a favored employee uses their influence and the impact it has on the overall team.

THE SCENARIO

Sherrie has been the leader of a finance team for the last eight years. Her organization has grown a great deal in that time and her team has seen a lot of change, including tons of turnover. The one thing that has remained consistent is Jess, one of her supervisors. Jess and Sherrie joined the organization within two months of each other and have been through a lot of challenging times, including operational adjustments and an ever-evolving team. They've also supported each other through a lot of life changes, like divorce and childbirth. No matter what, they have each other's back.

In a recent team engagement survey, Sherrie's overall team results aren't as high as she had hoped, particularly in the area of a hostile work environment and people feeling included. Several written comments highlight Jess specifically as a source of the problem. For Sherrie, this is frustrating because it isn't the first time these kinds of statements (for example, "I am scared of her," "She isn't open to other people's opinions," and "You don't want to get on her bad side") have come up. Over the years, many people who resigned had indicated Jess was a factor in their choosing to leave, for similarly stated reasons.

This always confused Sherrie, as she has never seen any indications of these behaviors from Jess. Jess has always written off such statements as simple miscommunication or coming from someone who was a bad fit for the team. Jess is a solid performer and gets results from her people. But now, HR is saying Sherrie needs to get to the root of this. Her turnover is too high for the size of her team, and these continued engagement scores are troubling. If she doesn't submit an action plan for resolution within a month, they will be getting involved and she might be placed on probation as an ineffective leader.

In a panic, Sherrie calls Jess into her office. As a leader on her team, Sherrie feels Jess has a right to know what is being said about her. Also, Sherrie really wants help about what to do from someone she trusts.

After looking over the documents, Jess states she has no idea where this is coming from but she will help Sherrie in any way she can. They decide Sherrie should conduct some interviews with various people on the team so she can hear from them directly. Once she has gotten to the bottom of these issues, it will all be okay.

Sherrie's first interview is with Jeremy, an analyst who has been on the team for a little more than a year. After explaining the purpose of the meeting, Sherrie encourages Jeremy to be honest so she can help create the type of team on which everyone feels safe and supported. He is hesitant at first but decides nothing will improve if people don't speak up, so he tells her the truth: Jess is very intimidating when Sherrie isn't around, and many people, including him, are somewhat scared of her. She is often openly dismissive in meetings, both verbally and nonverbally. At times, she constantly rolls her eyes when certain people (whom she clearly doesn't like) are speaking. Simply put, everyone tiptoes around her because, as a leader on the team, she can make life hard if you cross her.

Sherrie says she has never seen this behavior from Jess, and Jeremy replies that Jess only does this when Sherrie isn't around. At times, she even sabotages team members she doesn't like by "forgetting" to include them in key work meetings or by dropping them from email chains, which is why so many people keep leaving or asking for an internal transfer. The general feeling is people need to stay on Jess's good side because she has so much influence over Sherrie's decisions about the team.

Sherrie thanks Jeremy for his honesty—but follows that with "Not to be defensive, but" his characterization of Jess is off the mark and not who she is as a leader. He is wrong about her and he needs to work on this with Jess. Sherrie thanks him again for speaking so candidly with her and ends the meeting.

After Jeremy leaves, Sherrie is frustrated. His description of Jess is completely counter to the person she has worked with for so many years. The day only gets worse, as these same sentiments are shared by the other four people she interviews. Ultimately, Sherrie does what she has done for years: She calls Jess into her office to discuss the findings.

As Sherrie outlines what has been said, Jess becomes defensive and wants to know who said what. To be fair, she argues she should have the right to confront and address the issues directly with those making complaints. Sherrie, believing this is a justified request, shares the names and details of her conversations. She just knows this can be resolved if everyone can talk openly to each other.

The next morning, Sherrie has an urgent voicemail from HR, informing her of a complaint that has been made against her and Jess. An emergency meeting is set for later that morning. Sherrie is to come alone and not inform Jess of this communication.

Upon arrival at the meeting, the Human Resources

Business Partner (HRBP) informs Sherrie that, after her meeting with Jess the day prior, Jess had gone straight to confront Jeremy at his desk. In that confrontation, Jess demanded to know why he is scared of her. She also accused him of lying about her and added that she doesn't take kindly to liars.

Jeremy feels his confidentiality has been violated and Sherrie has created an environment that supports hostility and retaliation by telling Jess what he said. As Sherrie tries to defend Jess by saying it is likely just a misunderstanding, the HRBP states a witness overheard the whole conversation, so it is not to be disputed. The meeting concludes with HR saying an official investigation has begun and there will be additional meetings for her to attend. Also, they will be speaking with Jess immediately after Sherrie's meeting concludes to address next steps for her.

Let's begin the breakdown.

WHAT ARE THE TOXIC BEHAVIORS?

- Which parts of this story felt toxic to you?

  _____

  _____

- Which character did you think had the most toxic behavior in this scenario? Why?

  _____

  _____

- Where did leadership fail in this scenario?

  _____

  _____

- Where are there pivot points in this story when different choices could have been made for a different outcome?

  _____

  _____

- What would be the best next steps in this scenario to creating a safe team environment?

  _____

  _____

The dynamic between Sherrie and Jess provides many illustrations of how people who have worked together and are friendly can, at times, cross lines. It's important to remember that someone having toxic behaviors doesn't mean they are an unredeemable toxic person. They may have simply lost sight of what the right thing to do should be.

In this scenario, Sherrie definitely feels justified in her choices with Jess. But clearly she's ignoring the fact that Jess is creating a toxic environment in which people don't want to stay. What's not known here is whether Jess is intentionally using her influence on Sherrie, as the team believes. The reality is we don't know, but anyone can tell you that perception is often just as powerful and dangerous as reality. For this team, this dynamic is real and, therefore, it's not a safe environment for them if they're not in Jess's good graces.

One last note. When receiving feedback from someone, never start your response with "Not to be defensive, but," because whatever comes after this is just that: a defensive response. Our jobs as leaders are to listen to what our teams are trying to tell us, especially if what they are saying is difficult for us to hear. Listen. Thank them. Reflect. Don't respond emotionally and create a dynamic that subtly discourages candid discussion.

IMPACT

Let's walk through a few questions to think about how small behaviors create lasting impact.

- What would have made the team feel safe to speak freely?

  _____

  _____

- What was the impact of Sherrie giving all the details to Jess?

  _____

  _____

- What was the impact of Jess confronting Jeremy?

  _____

  _____

- Can a psychologically safe environment exist when there is a protected bully?

  _____

  _____

The impact of favoritism plays out here in an interesting, but not unique, way. Believing Jess has influence over Sherrie and Sherrie sharing details of her conversations, the team is right to feel unprotected. This sense of a hostile work environment and retaliation is clearly on display—if only Sherrie removed the favoritism blinders. Through her turnover and engagement surveys, her team is sending all the right signals. She is simply dismissing them because it doesn't align with her experiences or who Jess presents to her. This should have led Sherrie to be curious and to challenge her own objectivity.

This is critical for each of us to do. If information doesn't seem to match, take the time to first really challenge yourself with the facts. Maybe even seek out a trusted peer (who is not the leader in question) to talk it through. As leaders, it's our responsibility to not believe everything we think about those around us and to always try to maintain objectivity. By viewing Jess as a friend and not just a subordinate, Sherrie finds it harder to maintain the needed objectivity one must have as a leader. Again, we can never forget the power dynamics involved.

SELF-REFLECTION EXERCISE

Mirror time! Please take a few moments to really think through the following questions.

- With which person in this scenario did you most connect?

  _____

  _____

- What about this person or their actions hit home?

  _____

  _____

- When have you been guilty of playing favorites with your direct reports?

  _____

  _____

- What was the outcome of that?

  _____

  _____

- How do you feel about that situation now? Would you make the same choices?

  _____

  _____

- When have you been the recipient of favoritism?

  _____

  _____

- How do we, as leaders, remain objective when we have long-standing employees on our team whom we also consider friends?

  _____

  _____

I have already admitted I have both played favorites and benefited from being a favorite. Maybe not to the extent in the scenario in this chapter, but I have been given the benefit of the doubt when others might not have. It's important to admit if this is true for you. Frankly, this is what privilege is all about. It's when you are given advantages, for a variety of reasons, that aren't available to others. Just own it if this applies to you. It doesn't mean you aren't a hard worker. It simply means you may have had a few additional advantages.

The other thing I really want to speak to here is, like Cy Wakeman suggests, my favorites were most often tied to performance. Simply put, I like employees who show up and show out. I want to do great work and have a great team environment too. If you meet these criteria and don't bring in drama, I don't care who you are. I like you. Again, this may not feel good to the team members who aren't meeting those criteria, but it doesn't mean I am being unfair when evaluating performance. It's important to be able to separate crossing lines from simply rewarding desired behavior.

Gathering Thoughts

Let's start with favoritism. Loyalty and favoritism do not supersede actual work. Just because you like someone or someone has been a on team forever, doesn't mean it should affect your ability to hold them accountable and treat them fairly. There are many reasons why it's not best practice to be friends with a subordinate. Never confuse being friendly with being friends. At the end of the day, it's about business. Without the business, we wouldn't have jobs in the first place. Also, as leaders we are responsible for creating a safe workplace for *all* employees, not just the ones we like.

Let's dig deeper into the idea of being friends with your subordinates. Maintaining healthy boundaries and remembering the power dynamics among everyone you work with can be very challenging. The truth is we spend more time with people we work with than many of our family members and/or non-work friends. It makes sense that we develop deep and meaningful relationships at work. The hard reality is that the power dynamic between leader and subordinate can never be forgotten and is the reason why you shouldn't and can't be besties. You control their performance rating and compensation. You are simply asking for trouble by allowing blurred lines, and not maintaining some objectivity and really focusing on actual work and less personality.

Lastly, in the worst of situations, your favorite could

use or misuse your trust and relationship to their advantage. How many times have you heard someone name drop an influential leader and imply they can call to get what they want done? If you're anything like me, you'll be counting for a while.

Being a favorite creates a perceived shield of protection around their actions and words. I've always wondered if those leaders knew this was happening and how they'd feel if they did. Maybe some would care and some wouldn't, but the important thing is how this simple action creates an unbalanced work environment, introducing the haves and have nots. Those who can get away with things and those who can't.

I'd like to leave you with a challenge. Really take a look at where you are favoring people on your team today and ask yourself why. Is it because, like Cy Wakeman says, they are high performers and you want to reward and reinforce the right behaviors? Or is it because you have similar interests and/or feel more like friends? Is it because they look and act like you? Is it because you're very sympathetic and really want to be liked? Whatever it is, at least be truthful to yourself. Then decide: Is this the leader you want to be? Take your next steps accordingly.

CHAPTER 9

Can You Hear Me Now?

If you want to control someone, all you have to do
is to make them feel afraid.

~ Paulo Coelho

The Setup

We've all been in meetings when someone just drones on. Before you know it, you have no idea what's been said and, worse, someone is asking you a question. You are like a deer in headlights. Well, this chapter isn't about that. Quite the opposite.

Have you been in a meeting when people are disagreeing and someone appears to be getting upset? They're raising their voice to the point where people are shifting uncomfortably in their seats and are scared to make eye contact. I have. You don't know where to look, but you are scared to look anywhere, especially at the person who's on the verge of yelling. You would love to dig a hole in the floor and just get out of there. This is especially true when the screamer is your leader.

We, as leaders, set the tone, not just by the words we speak, but also how we speak them. I have taught leadership communication courses in which leaders would rate themselves as good communicators. However, many paused when asked if their teams would agree. In reality, most of us think we are great communicators. We also think we are funny. Chances are, we likely are neither most of the time.

When we think about different ways leaders communicate, the topic of screaming leaders is an interesting one. I've often asked people about their experiences with different leaders throughout their careers, and the results are mixed. Some people have never had a screamer in their midst. Those who have definitely have stories, and the similarities are interesting. First, screaming behavior tends to be accepted within the culture of that team, company, or even industry (I'm looking at you, food/restaurant industry). At times, it's just written off as the cost of doing business with a certain caliber of leader—almost as if it's a personality quirk or trait you just need to work around.

Ultimately, what everyone comments on is the resulting fear and intimidation that need to be accepted. If you can't take it, you leave. As long as the leader is good at getting things done, they stay. Even if turnover is high, if the leader can get results despite the retention issues, they are tolerated.

Now, I want to be clear about the difference between passionate assertiveness and bullying behavior. I have seen leaders become passionate, particularly in times of stress.

When speaking with lots of emotion, voices sometimes rise in volume but don't necessarily spark fear. Think of a coach's halftime speech in the locker room, rallying the players to believe in themselves. Or of a politician who is stumping on a topic that is close to their heart and using inflection to instill the same passion in those around them.

When a leader raises their voice in anger (or perceived anger) and it's directed at you in some manner, the dynamic changes. Being yelled at and fearing what will happen if you speak up or disagree is not a healthy dynamic or workplace. This is a textbook hostile or toxic work environment and a key reason why employees leave. Research has shown employees will not stay with companies in which toxic behavior is tolerated or rewarded.[16]

Let's take a look at a leader who is a screamer and sees this behavior as a strength.

SCENARIO

Like many female leaders, Alice has worked many years to finally be a senior director in her organization. Alice has thought of leaving because she is always being overlooked for promotions and ends up reporting to men who aren't as knowledgeable or skilled as she. Finally, she has reached the level she always knew she deserved.

Although she feels she is a great leader, she has been given feedback throughout her entire career that she's aggressive and loud. Words like *hostile* and *intimidating* are frequently used to describe her among subordinates and peers. She has even been offered executive coaching by the organization to help smooth out the edges. But Alice knows every tough woman gets told something like this. She is who she is, and she will demand the respect she is owed. No amount of leadership coaching will change her mind about how she will show up as a leader. Besides, some male leaders have told her that her loud voice is funny and quirky.

Alice knows her turnover is higher than other leaders', but it is because she is good at weeding out those who aren't really serious about the work. Besides, sometimes you have to be a bit tough to get things done. No one would ever say this to one of the male leaders in her company. They raise their voices all the time and no one tells them anything. They aren't labeled as intimidating. For them, it always seems to be described as passion.

Alice recently hired a director, Kelvin. He's new to the company as well as to her team but comes with extensive industry experience. Shortly after joining, he has people warning him Alice can be difficult to work with and to tread lightly. Don't get on her bad side or it could be lights out for him. He thinks these are pretty strong and implied sexist statements, and he decides to form his own opinion, as these comments feel pretty dismissive of his new boss. So far, she's been great to him and he is incredibly excited to get to work with her.

In a meeting with a support team to discuss a project kickoff, Kelvin sees a different side of his new boss. Alice starts to meet with some resistance from the other team when they don't agree with her ideas or approach to the project plan. As equal partners needed to move forward, it is important for all to be in agreement. Kelvin notices the volume of Alice's voice starts to get louder and louder until she is pretty much screaming at the other team. As this happens, the support team begins to speak less and less. Often, they share sideways glances of confusion and what appears to be outright fear. Ultimately, the meeting ends with only an agreement to meet again. Outside of introductions, Kelvin never says a word.

After the meeting, Kelvin is surprised to see Alice incredibly happy with the outcome. He expresses regret they weren't coming to a consensus on the approach, but Alice says his observations are inaccurate. The other team had indeed agreed with her. How could he not see it?

At this point, Kelvin is really shocked. He states they hadn't agreed but simply stopped disagreeing. Silence isn't necessarily agreement—to which Alice said, yes, it is to her. They had stopped talking because they knew she was right and agreed with her. With a serious and straight face, Alice tells Kelvin she finds when people disagree with her it helps to speak louder because they just aren't hearing her. Eventually, people finally hear her and agree with her approach.

Kelvin takes some time to reflect on all of this and decides to approach Alice. Very gently, he suggests the two teams haven't actually agreed on a plan. Kelvin reiterates to Alice that silence is not agreement. He also says he had thought she was actually angry with them because she was speaking so loudly. As a new person on the team, he simply wants to make sure he understands what she needs from him to be successful.

Alice is quiet for a while. She says just because she might be seen as yelling does not mean she was angry. She simply wants to make sure they are really hearing her. Further, she says this is needed, given that she is a woman. In her experience, women need to be a bit brash to get the attention required to be successful. As for whether there is agreement, it is on the other team to speak up. Otherwise, they are the weak ones.

She thanks Kelvin for having the courage to speak to her. They are a team, and she needs his support and trust to get things done. Kelvin walks away feeling a little better but still not great about her approach or how best to support Alice.

After the meeting, the other team reaches out to Kelvin to see if they can meet with him alone. They feel Alice isn't really open to other people's opinions and would like to hear his thoughts. Given he is new to the organization, they are hopeful he might have a fresh perspective and be open to the partnership. Kelvin is not sure what to do next.

WHAT ARE THE TOXIC BEHAVIORS?

- What are toxic behaviors demonstrated by Alice?

  _____

  _____

- How are toxic behaviors reinforced within this organization?

  _____

  _____

- Are there any elements suggesting the overall organization has a toxic culture? If so, what are they?

  _____

  _____

- What assumptions did you find yourself making in this scenario?

  _____

  _____

Yes, Alice is a screamer, and it has definitely created some challenges for her. These include turnover and strained peer relationships. In this scenario, it's encouraging to see her company identifies the challenges and has offered her professional development through the use of a leadership coach. However, one must be willing to make changes in order for that to be successful. Alice doesn't seem to be too receptive, especially since she's been rewarded through a promotion, and some executive leaders almost seem to encourage her style.

There's also the element of Alice feeling she must raise her voice to be taken seriously as a female leader, especially if she believes male leaders do the same with no repercussions.

Gender assumptions and stereotypes are definitely toxic, and it's a slippery slope to play into them. The truth is, based on the facts here, we don't know where this organization stands, but we should be asking the tough questions to ensure we aren't holding leaders to different standards.

The last behavior I want to call out is the partner team and their ask of Kelvin to go behind Alice's back, especially as a new employee. Instead of addressing the issue head-on, their approach actually adds complexity and drama to the situation. We all know people who've done this. Heck, we've likely been those people. Work around the obstacle rather than deal with the obstacle. It sets no one up for success, particularly Kelvin.

IMPACT

Let's walk through a few questions to think about how small behaviors create lasting impact.

- What was the impact of Alice's communication style?

  _____

  _____

- What is the impact of the support team reaching out behind Alice's back?

  _____

  _____

- What might be the impact of the project's success?

  _____

  _____

The impact on Alice's team is pretty clear: consistent turnover. People don't want to work for people who scream at them. Period. This will likely go for Kelvin too. Leaders lead by example and, so far, Alice's example is lacking, even if she brings redeeming skills and knowledge to the table. In this scenario, chances are the project will limp along and be completed, probably way after the due date and not in a team- or peer-friendly way. Feelings will be hurt, and there will be lots of meetings after the meetings, if you know what I'm talking about.

Ultimately, Alice is happiest and likely most successful when she has complete ownership of the project or direction. It's her word, with little counterpoint. Although she's been successful to this point, her style will eventually make it difficult to move up in leadership. Her biggest challenge will be herself.

SELF-REFLECTION EXERCISE

Please take a few moments to really think through the following questions.

- With which person did you most connect?

  _____

  _____

- What about this person most resonated with you?

  _____

  _____

- How would you describe yourself as a communicator?

  _____

  _____

- How would others describe you as a communicator?

  _____

  _____

- When have you felt bullied by someone's communication style?

  _____

  _____

- When have you bulldozed someone with your style?

  _____

  _____

- When has gender played a factor in how you judge a person's behavior?

  _____

  _____

- When have you felt your behavior judged for your gender?

  _____

  _____

- What biases do you have that might need to change?

  _____

  _____

Gathering Thoughts

I've had the privilege (not really) of experiencing leaders raising their voices in anger during team meetings and/or at specific individuals (including me). In these moments, it felt disrespectful and, quite frankly, scary. As professionals, we should expect more from our leadership, but unfortunately, we are human and some company cultures reward the wrong behaviors. When companies tolerate known screamers, they can't be surprised when turnover happens. Culture is critical to ensuring those bottom lines keep getting met. Fortunately, I was able to transition away from those leaders, but the reality is, not everyone is this lucky.

I also want to talk about gender differences and how this plays out in communication styles. I can't count the number of times I've heard an overly aggressive female leader say something like "They wouldn't say that about a man." Before I lose my lady card, I loudly admit there are different standards for men and women. However, this doesn't give female leaders the right to be pit bulls. You can be tough, but not sharp. You can be serious, without biting someone's head off.

I appreciate some industries require different strengths from all our leaders, but I would challenge every single person reading this, regardless of gender, to really ask themselves this question: Why do people follow you? Being successful in the past isn't always enough to keep a successful team in the future. People, especially now, demand more from their leaders.

I also imagine people might interpret a screaming leadership approach differently based on geographical location. Having worked in different parts of the United States, I can attest there are definitely cultural differences that tend to permeate into the workplace. However, I've experienced or observed screamers in various parts of the country and in various industries. Sometimes not in the ones you might expect, but they are there. I can also attest some industries and organizations tolerate this kind of behavior more than others. The impacts were always what you might expect: fear-based team culture and higher turnover.

Again, our teams deserve better than needing earplugs to survive the day.

CONCLUSION

"Everything you want is on the other side of fear."

~ Jack Canfield

I can almost hear the collective frustration out there. *"So, what am I supposed to do now?"* or *"Just tell me what to do when something like that happens."* Well, let me begin where we started and say there's no easy button for anything—especially leadership. There's no "Do this and everything will be perfect" answer because it simply isn't that easy. I don't know if there are any universal right answers, but there are definitely universal wrong answers. Hopefully, this book has helped you realize what a few of those are.

We know every person and situation is unique and has nuisances. You have to take what you know and apply some critical thinking to make your next move. To facilitate this, I ask you to complete one more reflection activity. I know some of these scenarios were gut-wrenching and likely brought up some tough emotions. It is important to not ignore these feelings and use them to help you grow into a better leader. So, one last time, let's walk through this together.

LOOKING BACK

- Which scenarios hit the hardest?
- Which negative emotions or experiences are you holding on to?
- What would you like to let go of?

LOOKING FORWARD

- What is one thing you have learned about yourself?
- What is something you would like to change going forward?
- How will you know if the changes are successful?
- What help will you need to make these changes?
- Who can be your accountability partner on this growth journey?

If you are struggling with what to change or where to start, the obvious answer is to go to those who know you well. When thinking about yourself, the only way to know how you're perceived is to ask in such a way that your team or peers can share feedback in a safe and comfortable way. This has to go beyond the traditional engagement survey that we know most team members are scared to answer honestly. Engage in a 360 review of a diverse group of subordinates, peers, and leaders by bringing in a third-party insight collector. Using a third party helps remove this fear. More importantly, you have to be open to whatever they tell you. You *cannot* be defensive; that defeats the purpose. The answers might hurt. And that's okay. We can't improve what we don't know.

Facing yourself in this manner is hard and can be draining, particularly if you don't like or agree with the answers. This work means embracing change, which we all know is difficult but must be done throughout our lives and careers. Staying stagnant is simply not an option. This means embracing fear and knowing you will get it wrong sometimes. No one likes to fail. I don't. I've worked my whole life to try to reduce risk and make smart choices. This is why it hurts so badly when I get it wrong. Doesn't mean I shouldn't keep trying.

Ask yourself, *"What bullshit am I bringing to this buffet?"*—every time you feel yourself getting drawn into a toxic scenario or getting emotional about a situation. It may be the most critical thing in helping you be the successful leader we both know you want to and can be. It's embracing the consistent journey of turning the mirror to yourself and understanding you are playing a role in this real-life scenario.

As I said previously, we all have skin in the game when there is drama or toxicity. I know this stings, but it's true. I've had to face my own role when looking at toxic situations in my past. There are things I may not be proud of, but I have learned who I don't want to be as a leader and remain aware of when I am getting drawn in.

Understanding we all have our baggage and are trying to do our best means missing the mark isn't always a failure. We can make big mistakes. As long as we acknowledge and learn from them, I don't think we should count this as failing. We are simply learning as we go by not falling into the same trap again.

This kind of work is so critical for leaders. We all need to be open and honest about our mistakes and how we are learning to be better leaders, peers, and overall people. Focusing on yourself shows you are vulnerable and leading by example. You are helping create future leaders who understand what it means to be human. Even the best leaders never stop getting better. If you do, there are implications to your team—and, ultimately, to you because people want to follow good leaders, not people who think they're perfect. Sometimes expressing fallibility is the most important thing a leader can do.

Just because I know it needs repeating, remember you are not alone on this journey. Reach out to those you trust. Mentors. Peers. Friends. Reach out to those who are able to share honestly with you when you are doing well and, more importantly, when you are missing the mark. They are here to help you succeed if you only are willing to ask.

I leave you with the one thing needed for all of this to work: *courage!* This is the most important value that guides my life. You need courage to do anything, but leadership really takes a special level of commitment. From growing yourself and managing the business to growing a team, there are challenges you can't imagine until you have experienced them. You hold people's careers in your hands, and this can never be taken lightly.

This continual self-development work isn't always easy and truly requires a thick skin. You must be willing to fail, publicly, and keep trying again the next day. I've been there and am still here. Thank you for joining me on this wild ride. I'll see you soon at the buffet.

DISCUSSION GUIDE

To prevent all you well-intentioned leaders who want to have healthy, productive discussions from falling into a toxic "book club gone wrong" death trap, I have created a group Discussion Guide for you. We have all been in a book club or discussion group before. For every amazing experience, I also have traumatic memories of discussions gone wrong. In an effort to facilitate productive insights, I thought it would be important to provide some resources to assist you.

Here are a few important rules to keep in mind when creating and leading an engaged group discussion.

1. **Understand the overt and covert political nature of the participants.** As a facilitator, ask yourself, "Will everyone feel comfortable sharing with others in the room?" If there is any hesitation on the answer, you have your answer. Be mindful of these dynamics as you facilitate the discussion.

2. **Have ground rules.** Be very clear about the objective of this group. There should be no finger pointing. This is about personal growth, not scoring points. People should be able to discuss freely without others in the group taking things personally or making assumptions. For this to happen, have the group create ground rules for the discussions. Remind them, as needed, to keep the discussions productive.

3. **Use the questions in this guide to spur conversation.** The self-reflection exercises throughout this book are meant to allow readers to dig deep into their personal experiences and reflect on these sensitive topics *in private.* These reflections are not necessarily meant to be used in a group discussion. This guide allows everyone to contribute without having to divulge anything too personal.

4. **Don't force people to share** anything from a personal experience they don't spontaneously offer. Especially with the topics we are broaching, it is understandable people may not want to share past traumas or mistakes. Allow participants to share what they feel comfortable sharing, when they want to share it. In the wrong environment, asking a reader to share intimate insights in a psychologically unsafe environment would result in the opposite effect of what a discussion like this is intended to do.

5. Thank participants for whatever is shared. **Acknowledge their bravery and courage.**

Now, on to the Discussion Guide.

Introduction

- Do most leaders know when they are being toxic?

- How often are you aware of your toxicity tendencies and how they show up to those around you?

- Do certain situations or people seem to bring

out the worst in you? In essence, just the idea of them stirs up the BS that you might bring to the buffet?

- Why is it easier to point the finger at others when viewing a toxic situation rather than consider our own role in what is happening?

Chapter 1: Toxicity and Why it Matters

- We covered different ways that leaders can be toxic. Are there certain kinds that feel more toxic? Why?

- Are you more forgiving of certain kinds of toxicity than others? Does it depend on the leader?

- What can we really do about toxic work cultures?

- When thinking of leaders you want to emulate, what is the one trait that you need to develop? What about something you believe is a leadership strength for you?

Chapter 2: I Swear it Wasn't Me

- What is the most difficult part about reflecting on some of your most challenging professional moments?

- Why is being vulnerable so scary?

- What have been your greatest growth moments so far on your professional journey?

Chapter 3: What's That Smell?

- What were some toxic elements in this scenario?

- What were the impacts of not addressing burnout? From a leader perspective? From a team perspective?

- How has burnout shown up in your company?

- What are some real coping mechanisms for burnout besides quitting?

- What are constructive ways for a leader to create a healthy team culture without falling into a "them versus us" mentality?

- What are safe and constructive ways of telling someone they are burned out and need a break?

Chapter 4: Walk the Talk

- What were some toxic elements in this scenario?

- Where were there pivot points when a different decision could have changed the outcome?

- How important is it for a leader to practice what they preach?

- What structure or rules allow open door policies to be used productively?

- Are there ever times when you should skip your direct leader and seek out a different or more senior leader when addressing a challenge?

Chapter 5: Fear and Loathing in the Office

- What were some toxic elements in this scenario?

- What are common mistakes that new leaders make when confronted with a challenging employee?

- How important is holding all employees accountable?

- What are good leadership responses to an employee who starts crying? What about screaming?

- Where should someone look for a mentor if they don't have a large network?

- What are the best tips for new leaders to consider when creating a culture of accountability?

Chapter 6: I'm Pretty Sure I Am God

- What were some toxic elements in this scenario?

- Considering this scenario, what steps can you take to learn more about a team culture prior to taking on a new role?

- What have you tried when you and your leader aren't seeing eye to eye?

- How do you onboard or treat new leaders in your company or on your team?

- How are you setting people up for success? Where could you do better?

Chapter 7: Where My Single People At?

- What were some toxic elements in this scenario?

- What are some general stereotypes that exist around single people?

- What about married people?

- What about parents?

- How do you check your own biases to insure equal opportunity for growth and advancement?

Chapter 8: You've Got a Friend in Me

- Which elements in this scenario might be considered toxic?

- Realistically, what do you do when a friend becomes a subordinate?

- How do you remain an objective leader in this situation?

- What are impacts of having a bully on the team?

- Can a psychologically safe environment exist when there is a protected bully on a team?

Chapter 9: Can You Hear Me Now?

- What were some toxic elements in this scenario?

- How important is a leader's communication style?

- Are there ever times when screaming is justified as a leadership approach?

- Are people of different genders viewed differently when they raise their voices?

- Instead of screaming, what other approaches could be used to achieve an objective?

Conclusion:

- What has been the biggest lesson you have gained from this book?

- What help might you need to address one of your toxic leadership tendencies?

- Who serves as your accountability partner when you want to make a change?

CHAPTER NOTES

1. "Toxic." *Merriam-Webster.* https://www.merriam-webster.com/dictionary/toxic.

2. D. Sull, C. Sull, and B. Zweig. "Toxic Culture Is Driving the Great Resignation." *MIT Sloan Management Review,* January 11, 2022. https://sloanreview.mit.edu.

3. Cy Wakeman. *No Ego: How Leaders Can Cut the Cost of Workplace Drama, End Entitlement, and Drive Big Results,* (New York: St. Martin's Press, 2017).

4. Ibid.

5. "Burn-out an 'Occupational Phenomenon': International Classification of Diseases." World Health Organization website, May 28, 2019. https://www.who.int/news/item/28-05-2019-burn-out-an-occupational-phenomenon-international-classification-of-diseases.

6. "Burnout." *Merriam-Webster.* https://www.merriam-webster.com/dictionary/burnout.

7. Wakeman, *No Ego.*

8. Brené Brown. *The Gifts of Imperfection* (Hazelden Information & Educational Services, 2010).

9. Christine Kane. "On Being Consistent (Even When You're Not)." Podcast audio. https://christinekane.com/podcasts/49/.

10. Sull, Sull, and Zweig, "Toxic."

11. Cy Wakeman. *Reality-Based Leadership: Ditch the Drama, Restore Sanity to the Workplace, and Turn Excuses into Results* (Jossey-Bass, 2010).

12. Sull, Sull, and Zweig, "Toxic."

13. Wakeman, *No Ego*.

14. Bella DePaulo. *Singled Out: How Singles Are Stereotyped, Stigmatized, and Ignored, and Still Live Happily Ever After* (St. Martin's Press, 2006).

15. Wakeman. *Reality-Based Leadership*.

16. Sull, Sull, and Zweig, "Toxic."

RESOURCES

Introduction

- Elizabeth Gilbert. *Big Magic: Creative Living beyond Fear* (2015).

Chapter 3: What's That Smell?

- Burnout Global website. https://burnoutglobal.com/

- "Burn-out an 'Occupational Phenomenon': International Classification of Diseases." World Health Organization website. https://www.who.int/news/item/28-05-2019-burn-out-an-occupational-phenomenon-international-classification-of-diseases

- Penny Reid quote. Goodreads website. https://www.goodreads.com/quotes/8759153-don-t-set-yourself-on-fire-trying-to-keep-others-warm

Chapter 4: Walk the Talk

- Brené Brown. *Dare to Lead* (Vermilion, 2018).

- Simon Sinek quote. Twitter. https://twitter.com/simonsinek/status/232556392114974721?lang=en

- Cy Wakeman. *Reality-Based Leadership: Ditch the Drama, Restore Sanity to the Workplace, and Turn Excuses into Results.* (San Francisco, Calif.: Jossey-Bass, 2010).

Chapter 5: Fear and Loathing in the Office

- Cy Wakeman. *Reality-Based Leadership: Ditch the Drama, Restore Sanity to the Workplace, and Turn Excuses into Results.* (San Francisco, Calif.: Jossey-Bass, 2010).

Chapter 6: I'm Pretty Sure I Am God

- Michael Maccoby. "Narcissistic Leaders: The Incredible Pros, the Inevitable Cons." *Harvard Business Review,* January 2004. https://hbr.org/2004/01/narcissistic-leaders-the-incredible-pros-the-inevitable-cons

Chapter 7: Where My Single People At?

- Judith Siers-Poisson. "How Single and Married Coworkers Are Treated Differently." Wisconsin Public Radio, June 14, 2017. https://www.wpr.org/how-single-and-married-co-workers-are-treated-differently

- Bella DePaulo. *Singled Out: How Singles Are Stereotyped, Stigmatized, and Ignored, and Still Live Happily Ever After* (St Martin's Press, 2006).

Chapter 8: You've Got a Friend in Me

- Victor Lipman. "A Common but Overlooked Management Problem: Playing Favorites." Forbes.com, January 16, 2018. https://www.forbes.com/sites/victorlipman/2018/01/16/a-common-but-overlooked-management-problem-playing-favorites/?sh=571d008235dd

- Reality-Based Leadership. "Why You Should Play Favorites at Work." November 2, 2017. YouTube video, 2:25. https://www.youtube.com/watch?v=pkjM3NtrDo4

ABOUT THE AUTHOR

Kimberly Benoit is a leadership coach, consultant, and best-selling author of *Entrepreneur Secrets: Coaches, Consultants & Experts Share the Secrets to Their Success*. She works with leaders and teams across all industries to confidently navigate needed change for continued success. Through a compassionate approach, she empowers them to confront the real issues and to create realistic next steps to move forward with confidence. She launched her business after an accomplished 24-year career as strategic and operational leader with expertise in program management, change management, crisis management, strategy development, and organizational effectiveness. Kimberly is active in the Project Management Institute (PMI) and the International Coaching Federation (ICF). She holds advanced degrees in clinical psychology and criminal justice. In addition, Kimberly is certified in the Mindful Leader's Mindfulness-Based Stress Reduction (MBSR) program and the Harrison Assessment. Kimberly, along with her sweet cat, Ruby, lives in New Orleans, Louisiana, and enjoys reading, cooking, listening to music, and traveling.

www.ingramcontent.com/pod-product-compliance
Lightning Source LLC
Chambersburg PA
CBHW051529120626
46551CB00012B/1146